COME,
WALK WITH ME

COME,
WALK WITH ME

**Lt. Col. Walter Dee Burnett
903 E. Main Street
Brownfield, TX 79316**

WALTER DEE BURNETT

A HEARTHSTONE BOOK
CARLTON PRESS CORP.
NEW YORK

Dedicated to you,
Dear Reader

CONTENTS

List of Illustrations ix
Preface xi
Introduction xiii
Acknowledgments xv
1. The Tour Begins 1
2. The Baptism of Jesus 5
3. The Cana Miracle 9
4. A New Birth 13
5. Miracle of the Name 15
6. The Fishes 17
7. Miracle of the Nobleman's Son 19
8. The Disabled Man 21
9. The Synagogue Demoniac 23
10. Peter's Mother-in-Law 25
11. Mass Healing 27
12. Cleansing the Leper 29
13. The Paralytic 31
14. The Withered Hand 33
15. The Centurion's Servant 35
16. The Widow's Son 37
17. The Stilling of the Tempest .39
18. The Two Blind Men 41

19. The Dumb Demoniac 45
20. The Gadarene Demoniac 47
21. Jairus' Daughter 51
22. Feeding of the Five Thousand 53
23. Walking on the Water 57
24. The Syro-Phoenician Woman's Daughter 61
25. The Deaf and Dumb Man of Decapolis 65
26. Feeding of the Four Thousand 67
27. The Bethesada Blind Man 69
28. The Transfiguration 71
29. The Demonic Boy 73
30. The Man Born Blind 75
31. The Infirm Woman 79
32. The Man with Dropsy 81
33. Raising of Lazarus from the Grave 83
34. The Ten Lepers 87
35. Blind Bartimaeus 89
36. The Withered Fig Tree 91
37. The Miracle of Malchus' Ear 93
38. At Calvary 97
39. Jesus' Crucifixion 101
40. The Resurrection 105
41. Post-Resurrection 109
42. Post-Resurrection Miracle of the Fishes 115
43. Jesus' Ascension 119
44. Peter Proclaims Jesus as Christ 121
45. How One Becomes a Christian 123
46. The Shroud of Turin 129
Postscript 133

ILLUSTRATIONS

Palestine in Christ's Time . . . . .xvii, 8
The Shroud of Turin 128

PREFACE

THIS BOOK IS MY missionary offering to those who have never accepted Jesus as their Lord and Savior. It is factual from the Bible.

I have always felt that if a person could "see" the miracles performed by Jesus that person would definitely believe in Him as the Son of God and the Lord and Savior of mankind.

God asked me to write this book.

The portrait of Jesus is an oil painting I did after having seen Him in a dream. I awoke and asked God to be with me as I painted. Even though I am a professional portrait artist, I felt unqualified to complete such an important commission. Ten months later, in March 1986, He and I finished the portrait.

Now Christ motions to you and says, "Come, walk with Me."

INTRODUCTION

PLEASE ACCEPT MY INVITATION to be your guide on a tour of the Holy Land. As a result of your close attention, you will be able to "see" for yourself. Try to use your mind's eye and you will "see" the characters of this time and their true story, and you will become involved in the plot. As through self-hypnosis you will travel back in time and will be able to "picture" the events as they happened, and you will be empathetic with your favorite characters as you "watch" their actions.

Your imagination will produce reality and be seen clearly in your consciousness. By using that wonderful mind-sight as I describe what is happening, you will be able to experience the evolution of Biblical New Covenant between God and man. Right before your eyes the documented miracles of Jesus Christ will happen. They are miracles performed by God through His Son, Jesus the King.

Jesus was placed on earth for a short period of time to tell and show how to live a happy existence by seeing, believing, and trusting in Jesus as your Lord and Savior. You will receive wonderful peace on earth, followed by a glorious and everlasting life with Jesus in Heaven!

Come, let us begin our tour.

ACKNOWLEDGMENTS

I AM INDEBTED TO the following for my reference sources:

The Daily Bible, in chronological order; Harvest House Publishers.

Description of Jesus: Guiding Light Edition, Holy Bible, Good Council Publishing Company.

News Reports of archeological discoveries.

Photographs: Books: The Shroud of Turin (1) by Ian Wilson, and (2) by Lynn Pickett and Clive Prince.

The Holy Bible, New King James Version, Copyright 1994, Thomas Nelson, Inc.

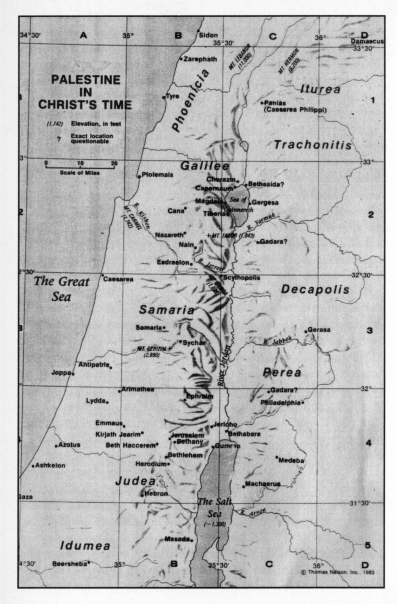

Palestine in Christ's Time
Where it all began

COME,
WALK WITH ME

1. THE TOUR BEGINS

I'M SO GLAD TO meet you, and to find out that both of us are headed for Jerusalem. I have been there several times and have even conducted tours for Americans from my Church. I am particularly glad that you have accepted me as your tour guide. We will have an enjoyable time, and it won't cost you anything! It will be my pleasure.

Well, at last we can board the plane and get under way. This airline company is small, but it is reasonable. That was what attracted me, and perhaps you also. Here, let's sit together so we can talk. It wasn't too bad having to wait a couple of hours until some repair work was done on the plane. Perhaps the rubber band under the hood had to be replaced.

How are you doing? I'm really surprised that this plane is not pressurized! Look, some of the older passengers have been fitted with oxygen masks. I don't know what our altitude is, but I hope we can make it all right over the Alps. Well, you and I seem to be breathing all right.

Look, we are going to make a stop at Damascus. This is where Saul was going when he was converted after a career of persecuting followers of Jesus. He was confronted by the voice of the resurrected Jesus in a blinding light. He and those with him fell to the ground. Paul, as he was named by Jesus later, was told by Jesus to go into Damascus and see a disciple who lived there, and do as he was told. As the result of much teaching there, Paul became an apostle of Christ to reach the Gentiles. Prior to that time, the religious emphasis was the conversion of only the Jews. I'm glad you and I were finally included by God.

Well, we didn't spend much time in Damascus, but we did have time to go in the airport gift shop. I'm glad I was able to get this little footstool shaped like a camel saddle.

We can see Jerusalem there below. See, it isn't far from some low mountains, but it is bordered on the west by arid land that becomes desert. Let's get checked into the International Hotel as soon as possible and get something to eat. I have stayed at this hotel many times and I like it. After dinner, in the quiet of our room, I would like to brief you on this city and its place in the history of Christianity.

Within its walls Old Jerusalem looks much the same as when Jesus was here. Many of the original adobe houses still remain. This town, and its people, played a very important role in Jesus' life, as you will see. Of course, Jesus' mock trial occurred here, followed by His dramatic crucifixion on the hill of Golgotha, and by the earthquakes, rain, and flood, with darkness in the afternoon by which God showed His anger. There on the cross Jesus bore all the sins of the world for all those who accept Him as Lord and Savior.

(Next morning) There, after that good breakfast, let us get started on our tour by walking in Jesus' footsteps. I have rented a car, so we will be able to get around quite well. Much walking, however, will still have to be done as we follow Jesus. I'm glad you have on some good walking shoes.

Ah, it's a good morning. Say, before we leave here, let's take a short stroll over there to the Garden of Gethsemane, one of Jesus' favorite places. Let this be the beginning of our tour. We will come back here toward the close of the tour, but first, I want you to begin to envision yourself in thought and action where Jesus walked before you.

See all these olive trees? The place looks essentially the same as when Jesus walked here. The olive tree lives a long time. You can imagine that some of these were here that night of great agony, distressful prayer, and bloody sweat. Imagine. Right over there Jesus knelt and prayed to His Father in Heaven while three of His disciples rested over there. They even dozed off while waiting. Once Jesus arose, He went over to them where they were supposed to be on watch. Jesus' Father assured Him that what was to happen was what had to be. He was filled with heavenly peace, even though He knew that soon He would die for mankind. He awoke the three and said, "Arise, let us be going."

Let your thoughts and apprehension be that which Jesus had that fateful evening. He was not afraid, ever, but He was sad-dened because He would be leaving His beloved friends, and the City of Jerusalem. The City which had not fully accepted Him as friend, Savior, or God.

As we drive along our way to Bethlehem, just observe the scenery, the area so well known by Jesus with its low hills and dusty roads. The first time I was here it rained, all five days I was here. I asked a native how much rainfall they had here in a year. "Well," he said, "it hardly rains more than five days."

My tour with you will mainly describe the many miracles performed by or for Jesus. His birth was the first one. Right here in the edge of this town He was born, not in a hospital or an inn. No, Jesus was born in a sheepherder's manger. Of course you have heard that before. The town was so crowded during tax time that no suitable place could be found for Mary and Joseph, so they had to stay where they could.

Jesus' birth was by a virgin through the Holy Spirit. In that moment of conception the Holy Spirit fused together both Deity and humanity into one supernatural being! At the hour of the Savior's birth a star made its appearance over the manger thus announcing the blessed event. Hovering just over the manger, that heavenly light pointed the way for shepherds from the nearby fields to follow and visit with baby Jesus. The star was high enough that it could be seen for hundreds of miles. God spoke to hearts, and people understood what was happening, and they wanted to believe. About three fellows, for example, saw the light from far east of Bethlehem, and they saddled their camels and headed out. They were so far away that it took great faith and about a year and a half to reach Bethlehem. By then Jesus was living in the city with His mother and stepfather. They eventually arrived, following the star in their hearts, and brought gifts of gold, frankincense, and myrrh, and they knelt before Jesus and worshipped.

Because of the seasonal change, the shepherds seldom kept their sheep out in the fields later than the end of October. So, it was about then that Jesus was born. The exact date is not significant since the fact that Jesus was born is the important point.

2. THE BAPTISM OF JESUS

(Matthew 3:16; Mark 1:9–12; Luke 3:21–23; John I)

VERY LITTLE IS KNOWN about Jesus during His childhood years. God had not planned for Jesus to begin His Ministry until He was full grown. Jesus was thirty years old, the age when Israeli men customarily embarked on a career, that He walked over to the Jordan River where He knew John the Baptist was. John saw Him approaching and his heart jumped with joy. They were related, and had no doubt played together as children, but now, suddenly, Jesus' true character became obvious to John. Jesus asked John to baptize Him. John was awestruck! He told Jesus that it was he that should be baptized by Him.

Jesus sought baptism by John on the basis of fulfillment of righteousness and to identify Himself with the expectation of the people with the customary demands. His life's task, or career, of devoting Himself to Messianic salvation began with the baptism.

John had always baptized with water, but he suddenly recognized Jesus as the Son of God, the One who would baptize with the Holy Spirit.

John was aglow with victory as Jesus emerged from the water, and he shouted, "Behold the Lamb of God, which beareth away the sin of the world."

Three things happened to the astonishment of those watching: the opening of the Heavens, the Voice of God, and the Holy Spirit descending like a dove to the shoulder of Jesus. All implied God's acceptance of Jesus' sinless existence and the anointing of Him with God's supernatural power and glory. The people there were astounded at hearing God's resounding Voice saying, "This is My Son of whom I am most proud!" What an experience to see the beginning of the New Covenant between God and mankind!

Right after the baptism Jesus desired to be alone. Having been commended by God the Father and endowed with the Holy Spirit, Jesus sauntered thoughtfully into the desert.

As we leave the Jordan River, let us continue our drive through the Holy Land. As we go along I want to talk to you about Jesus' existence and the many things that happened to Him. Please, now, in order to get the most out of this tour, divest yourself of all miscellaneous thoughts, and give concentrated attention to recorded events of His Ministry as they happen before your very eyes. Watch with your mind's eyesight.

The Devil appeared before Jesus there in the desert and tempted Him in an effort to destroy the Man of God. The temptations offered by Satan were not merely visions Jesus had but were real and intense. Jesus later described what was offered by the Devil, and His disciples were astounded and believed Him.

The three stages of temptation were directed to "distrust," "presumption," and to "worldly sovereignty." In each case Jesus rejected the temptation because He knew that He must always be victorious over the strength and subtlety of the Devil. First, because Jesus had remained in the desert for many days without any food, and His physical being was so hungry, the Devil told Him to convert the desert stones into bread. Jesus ignored the suggestion. Then the Devil carried Him to the pinnacle of the Temple telling Him that He could throw Himself off and not be hurt. Jesus didn't comply, but He didn't stop the Devil in his tempting. He wanted to see how far the Devil would go. Lastly, from atop a mountain the Devil showed Him all the kingdom of the world and its glory. He told Jesus that He could have it all in the flash of a moment. Rejecting that also, Jesus walked out of the desert with the power and elegance of the Holy Spirit.

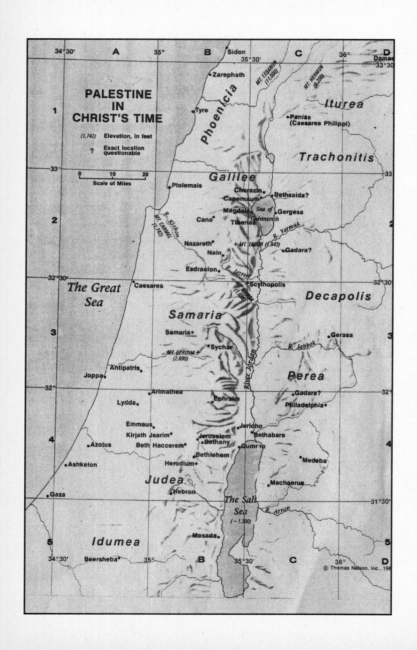

PALESTINE IN CHRIST'S TIME

(1,742) Elevation, in feet

? Exact location questionable

0   10   20
Scale of Miles

Damas

Sidon
35°30'
33°30'

Zarephath

MT. LEBANON (11,000)

MT. HERMON (9,200)

Iturea

Tyre

Phoenicia

Panias (Caesarea Philippi)

Trachonitis

Galilee

Ptolemais

Chorazin
Capernaum
Bethsaida?

Magdala
Sea of Gennereth

Gergesa

Cana
Tiberias

R. Kishon

MT. CARMEL (1,742)

R. Yarmuk

Nazareth
+ MT. TABOR (1,843)
Gadara?

Nain

Esdraelon
R. Jezreel

The Great Sea

Caesarea

Scythopolis
32°30'

Decapolis

Samaria

R. Jordan

Samaria
Sychar

MT. GERIZIM + (2,890)

R. Jabbok

Gerasa

Antipatris

Perea

Joppa

32°

Gadara?

Arimathea

Philadelphia

Lydda

Ephraim

Emmaus

Jericho

Kirjath Jearim
Jerusalem
Bethany
Bethabara

Azotus
Beth Haccerem
Bethlehem
Qumran

Ashkelon

Herodium

Medeba

Judea

Machaerus

Gaza

Hebron

The Salt Sea (−1,300)

31°30'

R. Arnon

Idumea

Masada

Beersheba
35°
35°30'
36°

© Thomas Nelson, Inc., 196

3. The Cana Miracle...The First by Jesus

(John 2:1–11)

COME NOW AND LET us go with Jesus. As you and I walk with Him you will become involved and have empathy with Jesus and some of the people we will see. The documented miracles performed by Jesus are true and will appear right before your eyes. You are empowered to live and walk wherever He goes. Though we are dressed differently and we drive from one major location to another, we cannot be seen. We are blessed in that we can see but cannot be seen, we can hear but not be heard, We can walk, follow Him and believe the truth.

Leaving the desert landscape, victorious over the Devil, Jesus walked back to the town of Cana in Galilee, just a few miles west of the Sea of Galilee. The official name of the lake is Chinnereth, but they don't call it that. Yes, He has come down from the "Mount of Temptation." Look, it seems as if all of the town has been invited to a wedding. The celebration is being set for a boy and girl of prominent parents, and possibly one of the two is a distant cousin of Mary, the Mother of Jesus. Some of the first few disciples have already arrived and are seated over there. Look, Jesus has gone over to them and sat down with them on the grass. The "Son of Man," as He was often referred to later, was never ascetic, and He eats and drinks like everyone else. The documentation of this event states that "Christ adorned the marriage by His presence." It was fitting that the Lord of Life appeared joyous at the feast since He always came to sanctify all human life.

Look at what is happening! Having so many guests at the party has brought on a shortage of wine. Mary, sensing the need and feeling somewhat embarrassed, goes over to Jesus and whispers. "They have no more wine!" She felt that He could do something about it. Jesus calmly rebuffed her. On a couple of other occasions she had intruded into the Lord's domain and Jesus had rebuffed her tenderly each of those times.

The wine pitchers were virtually empty as were the water pots in the feast chamber. Finally, at Jesus' command, the servants filled the pots with water. Would you look at that, the water has turned to wine, and of such excellent quality as to call forth high praise from the master of the feast. He called it "...the best wine." And the guests think so, too! He who would not work any miracles during the Devil's temptations to meet His own needs, supplied a luxury for the wedding guests.

As you noticed, Jesus did not touch any of the vessels, but had merely asked the servants to pour water into them. By His divine power He simply willed the instant chemical change whereby water became like aged wine mellowed with keeping.

This miracle "manifested forth His glory." Exhibited here was the creative power essentially belonging to a deity. Shown to all present was the glory of His beneficent grace. His disciples were very impressed and they believed in Him even more so.

What we have seen here has been only one of the hundreds of miracles performed by Jesus Christ. Some of these we will see with our mind's eye are documented, and are typical of apostolic recognition of the extent of Jesus' Divine powers. The apostle John said this about Jesus' miracle ministry:

"Many other signs (miracles) therefore did Jesus in the presence of His disciples, which are not written in this book.... There are also many other things which Jesus did, in which, if they should be written every one, I suppose even the world itself could not contain the book that would be written." *(John 20:30; 21–25)*

4. A New Birth

(John 3:1–6; Peter 1:23; James 1:18)

GOOD MORNING! I HOPE you slept well. Ready to follow Jesus? As we drive over to witness the next event let me fill you in with some background information. Nicodemus, a fine product of Judaism, was very curious about Jesus; who He was, what were His objectives, and so forth. As a member of the ruling class, the Sanhedrin, Nicodemus had examined the credentials and record of John the Baptist. Now he wanted to know fully about Jesus because he felt from his study that this new teacher had really come from God.

Well, after finding out where Jesus was staying that night, Nicodemus went to Him after dark for a personal, undisturbed interview with Him.

During the discussion Jesus informed the well educated and religious man of the necessity of "a New Birth." Listen to this. "Man, born in sin and living in sin, must be reborn."

Nicodemus asked, "How can a man be born when he is old?"

Jesus says, "As there can be no entrance into the Kingdom of the flesh save by natural birth, so there is no entrance into the Spirit life save by a spiritual birth. That which is born of the Spirit is Spirit."

Nicodemus looked startled at first at the idea of a birth from

Heaven. Christ symbolizes the Spirit as a free, irresistible, invisible wind. The wind of Heaven is unlimited to race, age or sex.

What a miraculous event it is when God takes a poor sinner and makes him or her into a new life simply because God is asked, by believing in Him, to forgive all his sins.

Nicodemus and Jesus discussed miraculous truths of regeneration and redemption that are only possible through Him, God, and no other way. Yes, Nicodemus learned of the New Covenant. Though such regeneration of life is invisible, it becomes visible in the person's transformed life in which old things pass away and all things become like new. Yes, it is like being reborn! What an amazing concept!

Nicodemus went away walking like a New Man.

5. Miracle of the Name

(John 1:1–14)

O N OUR WAY TO the lake in Galilee let me tell you more about Jesus, and about what His name really means.

Christ is presented to humanity as the Word of God. "In the beginning was the word, and the word was with God, and the Word was God." *(Genesis 1:1)* Christ's name is called the "Word of God." *(Revelation 19:13)* As the Word, He, Jesus Christ, came as the revelation of the Father's mind, *(John 14:8,9)* Words, like expression of thoughts through Christ are God's thoughts, intents, meaning, and directions. They are made intelligible to us so as to be clear to the human mind.

Jesus Christ said, "The Father and I are one." *(John 10:30)* Such stated equality with God was hard to accept by the religious leaders when Christ was on earth. They rejected Him, and they tried to stone Him. God, the Father of all creation consequently created "God the Son, our Lord, the person through which the creative purpose moves. Through Him the infinite God utters Himself in His Words." *(Revelation 4:11)* Thus the further development of His Religion evolved as the New Covenant through Christ, the Word of God the Father. Through Him, Jesus Christ, religion was refined as "Christianity," the New Covenant of God with man.

15

6. THE FISHES

(Luke 5:1–11; Matthew 4:18–22; Mark 1:16–20; John 1:35–43)

YOU SEE, AS JESUS' fame grows, He is followed by crowds wishing to know more about what He is preaching. Look at that crowd assembled near Him by the sea of Galilee. It is here that the ancient prophet Isaiah said would be the location of much beneficial activity of the Messiah. *(Isaiah 9:1,2)*

Look, Jesus is so pressed by the people that He gets on the bow of a fishing boat, which, as it turns out, belongs to a fellow named Simon Peter. He can teach better from that vantage point. So, after teaching for a long spell, He turns to the owner of the boat and says, "Launch out into the deep, and let down your nets for a draught."

Peter's reply is characteristic of the big fisherman, "Master, we have toiled all night, and have taken nothing." But somehow the command by Jesus made him think, and then he replied, "Nevertheless, at Thy word I will let down the net."

You can see that Peter considered it a useless effort, so he let down only one net. Yet, look at that! There is such an immense draught of fish straining the net that Peter has to seek help from his fishing partners in the other boat in order to haul in the catch! That command, of such a King, was so authoritative, had so much implied power, that even the fish of the sea obeyed His will. Peter, and all of us watching, are profoundly moved by the miracle performed by the Sovereign Ruler of all things.

This miracle, and all miracles done by Jesus, are so incredible that we, with our limited ability to understand, are incapable of believing at first. Being able "to see" the events, however, enables us to better understand His Godly powers. We humans always look for reasonable logic in all happenings. Christ, as God, is beyond the laws of logic.

This particular miracle occurred in the beginning of our Lord's ministry. Peter, standing in front of Jesus, bowed his head and said, "Depart from me, for I am a sinful man, O Lord." In seeing such evidence of the Lord's glory, Peter saw his own evil heart, and his own ineptitude.

This miracle in Galilee gave Jesus opportunity to call Peter and his crew into discipleship. Jesus said to them, "Henceforth thou shall be fishers of men." Andrew, James, and John left their boats, their nets, and all those fish; they even left their homes, right then, and walked away with Jesus. After such a display of power, the fishermen knew that the One who had just called them to full-time service could meet their every need. Look, their faces are flushed with joy.

7. MIRACLE OF THE NOBLEMAN'S SON

(John 4:46–54)

WE HAVE SPENT A couple of days in the vicinity of Cana and now we see Jesus coming into view. He has spent a couple of happy days among the Samaritans who believe in Him. Here in the Cana area Jesus has spent much time with His new disciples and has knit Himself into a closer union with them. News of Christ's miraculous ministry has traveled fast. Among those attracted is that nobleman from Capernaum. See, on the map on page 8, Capernaum is at the upper northeast corner of the Lake of Galilee. This distressed father, whose son was at death's door, has ridden to Cana to ask for help from the miracle-worker. From what he had heard, he had gained the beginning of "faith." In all His healing miracles Jesus has taken utmost care to evoke faith from those He heals. You will see that He teaches that the miracle is not the cause of faith so much as its reward; that belief in Him as a healer is meant to lead to faith in Him as the Savior.

As we watch, the nobleman asks Jesus to "come down (to his house), ere my child will die." Of course he could not realize that the One whose help he seeks is able to heal just as easily from a distance as in person. Christ rebukes him, "Except ye see signs and wonders, ye will not believe."

The Lord knew with certainty that the nobleman's faith was

limited and weak. He nurtures that faith. Christ tells him, "Thy son liveth."

Later we will hear that on the way home, the nobleman's servant came running to meet him and tells him the happy news that his son has been healed. Yes, it happened at the exact moment when Jesus said, "Thy son liveth."

Look at the things this miracle accomplished. It healed the boy, and it also healed the father of his lack of faith. As a result of it all, the nobleman's whole household became believers in Christ.

8. The Disabled Man

(John 5:1–4)

L ET US FOLLOW JESUS on this Saturday morning, the Sabbath or Holy Day. We can be sure as we walk with this group of people following Jesus, that something wonderful will happen. From what we have seen, we can expect much more. We are approaching the Pool of Bethesda. It is located on the east side of Jerusalem where some intermittent spring operates. As usual, there are some crippled men near the pool. The word "Bethesda" means "place of mercy or compassion." In a few years from now this pool will become known as "The Fountain of the Virgin." When the water moves, it seems to have a peculiar power; a healing ability seems to impart new energy to the blind or the lame. It has long been the popular belief that God exercises His healing power through the rippling of the water.

Look, there are five porches, or benches, set around the pool for the invalids. Some religious leaders, who revel in the scriptures, contend that the five porches represent the five books of Moses, or the Law. The sick man there that Jesus now walks toward has been so withered and weak that he cannot get in the water by himself before the water stops rippling! Look, is Jesus going to lift the man into the water? The healing is only effective during the brief, intermittent rippling! Crippled for thirty-

21

eight years, the poor man still has remained hopeful when brought to the pool. Jesus, the omnipotent One, undoubtedly knows the man's medical history without being told, so He asks the man, "Wilt thou be made whole?"

"Sir," he replied, "I have no man, when the water is troubled, to put me into the pool."

Jesus, looking into the man's eyes, pitying the poor man's helpless condition, assists him to have renewed hope and faith, which He requires of the man. The old fellow knows he cannot move enough by himself, yet, he feels the command of omnipotence as Jesus says, "Rise, take up thy bed, and walk." His command is the enabling power for the impossible! The cure is instantaneous, complete and free, like the Spiritual restoration Christ supplies when a sinner is saved.

Look, the healed one takes a deep breath of relief, rises to his feet, stoops and picks up his poor rag pallet, and starts walking away. Isn't that something to see!

Christ did not come to heal all the crippled bodies around the pool, but rather to annex the demonstrated healing with the truer healing of soul and spirit. What a revelation!

When the members of the Sanhedrin hear of this, they will have no exhilaration over the poor man's relief and happiness. They are appalled at Christ's act of healing on the Sabbath, an unlawful act. That miracle begins the open conflict between Jesus and the religious rulers which will eventually finalize at the cross some two years later. Acting as One claiming authority from God, Jesus rebukes His foes for not accurately interpreting the scriptures, or not understanding their reference to Him, the Messiah.

Later there develops six other recorded healing miracles done on the Sabbath. The one we just witnessed was the first.

A few days later the Healer and the healed met in the Temple. The recovered poor man expresses his thanks to Jesus, and furthermore, confesses openly the wonder of it all to the foes of Christ.

Jesus tells him, "Behold thou art made whole; sin no more, lest a worse thing come unto thee;"

Doubtlessly the man will go forth whole in soul, as well as in body.

9. The Synagogue Demoniac

(Luke 4:33–36)

As was His custom, Jesus always goes to the Synagogue where He read and teaches. The congregation always listens in astonishment. On this day while we watch, the service is suddenly disturbed by the outburst of a demon-possessed man. Of course Jesus' discourse is interrupted by the shriek of the man, and the quiet of the sanctuary is greatly upset!

A demon of the Devil had invaded the personality of the man. While such possession may be inexplicable to you and me, it did happen right before us.

"What have we to do with thee?" he shouts!

Christ rebuked not the man, but the demon possessing him. He says, "Hold thy peace," (meaning "shut up.") He then gave the evil spirit a short, direct order. Speaking sharply, He says, "Silence! Come out!"

Obedient to higher authority, the demon does not speak further, although it does cry out in a loud voice, an inarticulate utterance of rage and pain! Can you imagine this? The Devil, however, shafted over his relinquishing control of the one he possessed, had done all the harm he could. The Devil throws the man down in terrible convulsions! He is hurled with a convulsive leap into the midst of the astonished congregation, and

is left prostrate but unhurt. Christ has delivered the man free
of the Devil's presence.

As the result of Christ's authority over unclean spirits, the
people are all amazed. Such a display of supernatural power is
new to them, and to us. What a sight! The people who witnessed this with us are overwhelmed! Christ just sounded the
death knell of Satan's domination.

10. PETER'S MOTHER-IN-LAW

(Luke 4:38–40; Matthew 8:14–17; Mark 1:29–31)

Here, let us follow Jesus and Peter, and others, over to Peter's house in Capernaum. We have just left the Synagogue after the healing incident of the demon possessed man. That was amazing, but now I'm glad it's over with. Peter's wife has her mother with her and she is sick. Christ is walking slowly. He wants a little rest and refreshment. There are already some people in the house. Look, some of them are asking Jesus to do something for the mother. Maybe it's nothing serious. This is in the spring of the year when fevers are common. Luke, the Doctor disciple, just told Jesus that she has a "great fever." Well, Jesus just walks into the room where the elderly lady lies on the bed, and He "rebuked" her fever. Just like that, He takes her by the hand and lifts her up. Yes, the fever is gone!

As you may know, the touch, or the laying on of hands, is a specific action of curing. Jesus even laid His hand on lepers, though never, as far as is known, upon demoniacs. Through those hands flows that supernatural energy, producing a direct and immediate cure. Christ infused the woman with full strength, enabling her to be up and about. She is not in a weakened condition! No convalescence is necessary in her case. What appreciation she has, and she shows it by preparing food and drink for Jesus and the others.

11. MASS HEALING

(Luke 4:40–41; Matthew 8:16,17; Mark 1:32–34)

AMAZINGLY, THE TWO MIRACLES we just saw, and the one we are going to witness here, all occurred on the same historic Sabbath day. The news of the Synagogue miracle and that of Peter's mother-in-law traveled fast. At sunset outside Peter's house, a large group of people has arrived so that it seems like a hospital waiting room. See, the miracle of the demonic has encouraged people to bring all the demon-possessed they can round up. Others brought all ailing persons they knew of so that they could also be healed. Well, in the cool of the evening Jesus continued His healing mission far into the night. Jesus healed them all, imposing upon each a vow of silence concerning His identity as the Messiah. Can you believe what you are seeing? Many, many people have been made joyously happy, and those who brought them, as they walk away from the front yard. Christ had laid his hand on every one of them, and they were all healed.

Well, we had better be getting on our way. What a day this has been in the town of Capernaum! No sufferer, individual of the crowd, ever was denied the healing compassion of Jesus. Such miracles are looked upon as fulfillment of prophesy. "Himself took our infirmities and bare our sicknesses inasmuch as He bore mortal suffering life, in which He alone could bring them to an end, and finally swallow up death, and all that led to death, in victory!!!"

12. Cleansing the Leper

(Matthew 8:1–4; Mark 1:40–45; Luke 5:12–15)

LEPROSY WAS A LOATHSOME, pitiful disease, so prevalent when Christ was on earth. It was nothing short of a living death, a poisoning of the very spirit of life. Little by little the body would decay and fall away. Under the old dispensation lepers were declared unclean and no medical means of treatment was available for their cure or relief. Because of the nature of the disease Christ's divine mission took on a peculiar and added force.

The Jews called leprosy "the finger of God," or "the stroke," indicating that the disease was regarded as a direct punishment by God and absolutely incurable. Look over there, Luke is now telling Jesus about that man standing nearby.

"He is full of leprosy," he tells Him.

In those days lepers had to live apart from all others, and to wear an outward sign of separation on their brow, and to cry out the words of warning, "Unclean, unclean!"

This leper has approached Jesus and "fell on his face," the highest display of homage. He has shown true reverence in the presence of the One he called "Lord." The leper's hope of finding cleansing at the feet of Him whose powers are unlimited is done through faith. We, today in our world, accept the truth of

His Lordship and there is no difficulty in crediting Him with almightiness. The common objection that miracles are inconsistent with the laws of nature is beside the point when it refers to Jesus. Since miracles are sovereign interpositions of the Lord, they are altogether apart from, and above, the laws of nature.

"Thou canst make me clean," the leper implored. "If thou wilt." No doubt he fears that Jesus might hesitate to stop and touch one so unclean. As he felt that his foul disease was believed to be the result of sin, would He pity him and "cleanse" him? Mark told us later that as the Lord looked at the leper He was "moved with compassion." Others, meeting a leper, would draw back in horror and evade him. But the Lord was touched with deep feeling because of the man's infirmity. He touched him! Under the Mosaic Law, to touch a leper meant defilement and social death. With the Lord of life and the conqueror of death, however, it is different. As the Healer and Savior of men, He stretches out His hand—now watch this—and touches the leper! The man is immediately cleansed! Instantaneously the leprosy disappears, and the skin is made whole! The sores are closed and the once foul flesh takes on the tints and tones of robust health! Amazing!

Christ imposed silence, as was customary, regarding the cleansing of the man, and said, "Tell no man!"

Mark then said that He "Straightly charged" him, or vehemently urged him to say nothing about the cure. That was a silence that no man could keep! His appearance had changed, and he was so happy, that he, as with all the others who were asked not to tell, just "had" to tell everybody he could. Christ told the healed man to show himself to the priest and offer a gift for a testimony. He did that and thus fulfilled the requirement of the law as to his fitness to return to normal life. (Leviticus 13:14) But then, because the man shortly broadcast his cure, Jesus was forced to seek retirement to desert places, for if all lepers heard about the healing they would flock to Jesus in mass.

13. THE PARALYTIC

(Luke 5:18–25; Matthew 9:2–7; Mark 2:3–12)

WELL, HERE WE ARE back in the town of Capernaum after the cleansing of the leper out in the country yesterday. This city adopted Jesus after He and His family left Nazareth, the home of His childhood. Jesus always liked Capernaum, particularly after His rejection by the Nazarenes. *(Luke 4:30,31)*

We are back in Peter's house. Look at the crowd of people around the front of the house and looking in the windows. Around here toward the back, yes, there is Jesus inside the back room. Christ, the teacher, is proclaiming to Pharisees, scribes, and peasants the truths of God.

It is late afternoon. Look, four men are carrying a friend, a poor paralytic on his bed, but they can't get in to see Christ because of the throngs of people. They are determined to get their "palsied" friend into the circle of healing and teaching somehow. Such determination is strong evidence of their faith. Necessity, being the mother of invention, has led to a novel method of getting the bedridden man upon the roof. They have come around and laboriously climbed up. Look, they have ripped off a section of roofing. Then, using rope, they are lowering the man down to where Jesus stands! You notice how the crowd of people stare up at the bold action. Jesus' teaching has to wait. The Pharisees and scribes are suspicious as to what might happen next. Jesus seems unperturbed and not offended by the intrusion. It is the faith of the four friends which Jesus honors rather than any faith the sufferer may have had.

How astonished the people seem when they hear Jesus say, "Son, be of good cheer, thy sins are forgiven thee." You see, Christ, exercising His divine prerogative, has forgiven the man of his sins, thereby fulfilling the prophesy of old, "Who forgiveth all iniquities." *(Psalm 103:3)* His enemies thereabout immediately cry out, "What blasphemy! He professes to forgive sin, a right which belongs to God alone!" Understanding that the forgiveness of sin is a divine prerogative, those blind scribes fail to see that Jesus is God manifest in the flesh.

Jesus always has the divine faculty of perceiving their thoughts. To Him they are as open as a scroll to Him who can read the hearts of all men. Giving voice to the inner thoughts of the scribes, Jesus says, "Which is easier to say, your sin is forgiven, rise up and walk?" The man did just that, he picked up his bed and walked, and the crowd, which had blocked his way before, now step back and allow him to walk out, with a cleansed soul and a thoroughly healed body. Although this wonderful miracle amazed the people, it only further irritated the blinded Pharisees, making them even more determined to destroy this man who chose to make himself equal to God.

14. THE WITHERED HAND

(Luke 6:6–10; Matthew 12:9–14; Mark 3:1–6)

WELL, ON THIS DAY let us drive back up to Galilee. Let me point out to you the staggering number of miracles we have witnessed in such a short time. As John said, if all the miracles of Jesus had been recorded, no book would have been able to hold them. Just to be fair about what Jesus did, let us stay with the truth, without adding conjecture or change.

Shortly after His return to Galilee, it seemed as if He had become involved in fresh disputes with the Pharisees about the constant contention concerning Sabbath-keeping. Well, on this day Jesus sees a man in the synagogue with a withered hand. You can see Jesus' antagonists are nearby and they are watching Jesus closely, always expecting our Lord to heal the afflicted man at any time. They are set to entrap Him again in regard to healing on the Sabbath. They have already resolved that, if He does heal, they will make it grounds for a definite accusation before the local tribunal *(Matthew 5:21)*.

In His masterly way, Jesus answers the traditionalists by citing their own practice of permitting the rescue of a sheep that had fallen into a pit on the Sabbath. He asked them, "Is it lawful on the Sabbath to do good, or to do harm, to save a life or to kill?" an obsequious reference to the murderous intent of the

Pharisees even on a Sabbath day. When Jesus sees the man with the withered hand, you can see that His heart of compassion goes out to him. This presented an opportunity to prove that a man is more important than a sheep.

Jesus looked about Him with the flashing in His blue eyes, because of the hardness in their hearts. The way that He felt at their sinful attitude resolved itself into pity and compassion toward the men who were guilty of it.

Jesus says, with authority, "Stretch forth thy hand." The man was told to "stand forth," in other words he is ordered to stand in view of all present so they could witness the miracle. Look at this! As the man raises forth his hand it is no longer dried up, but is perfectly restored and healthy like the other hand.

The Pharisees are "filled with madness," a senseless rage absent from logical reasoning. Inflamed with their hate, the Pharisees, along with the Herodians, take council as to how they can destroy Jesus. They had no qualms of conscience in plotting to kill on the Sabbath. They knew their intentions. This is one of the eleven recorded instances when Jesus will withdraw to the solitary hills away from His enemies. There He communes with His Father and takes time to choose the remainder of the twelve disciples who will be His witnesses subsequent to His ascension.

Here you and I see the forceful illustration of the character of faith. The order "stand forth" tests the courage of the man's faith. It rose above fear. "Stretch forth thy hand" tested the deeper quality of his faith, that of trusting Jesus completely.

15. THE CENTURION'S SERVANT

(Matthew 8:5–13; Luke 7:1–10)

As we head back to our hotel, let me tell you about the healing of a centurion's servant. Now it can be pointed out that Christ can and does cure illnesses from a distance and in the absence of the sufferer through the medium of the spoken word. Four of the disciples report such happenings. Luke, as a Gentile, wrote for Gentile's information and, therefore, omits the warnings to Israel, but introduced instead the aspect so instructive and encouraging to that race that the centurion, in the first place, persuaded the Jewish elders to plead for him with the Lord.

Luke tells us that this miracle was performed one day when Jesus came into Capernaum. The centurion's servant was so sick that he was on the verge of dying. The word Luke used for "servant" was "slave," yet he was not treated as a common or paltry person, or chattel as the term was applied in those days. This "slave" was more like a son to the centurion. He was dear and precious to his master. The officer was a commander of a hundred soldiers, yet he blended affection with authority.

To Jesus he said, "Say in a word, and my servant shall be healed." What a sincere proof of the centurion's faith is thus revealed! By faith he felt that distance was like nothing to Jesus, that His word at a mile's distance would cure as well as actual presence and touch. Here was a man of authority believing that disease had to obey our Lord's bidding just as those in his command had to obey him.

As soon as Christ heard of the plight of the slave and beheld the humility of the centurion, He said, "I will come and heal him,"

Someone then ran on ahead and told the centurion that his request was to be granted. The centurion had returned to await Jesus' arrival. When the officer had been told by the runner, and he believed, complete healing occurred. This miracle shows how the principle of faith is supreme over all privileges of race and birth. When the centurion arrived at home and found his servant as well as ever, he was supremely elated. His other household members told him just when the cure happened and, astonishingly, it happened at the very time of day when Jesus said, "I will heal him." How about that!

16. THE WIDOW'S SON

(Luke 7:11–18)

O N THE NEXT DAY after the healing of the servant there occurred a mightier and more wonderful miracle. Jesus had left Capernaum and had arrived in "a city called Nain," about five miles southeast of Nazareth. Two groups of people had met outside the town's cemetery. Jesus, with some of His disciples and interested followers, joined with the crowd of mourners gathered there for the funeral. This seemingly incidental meeting was held in the councils of divine providence. This meeting of the two crowds of people must have been impressive. The result? Life triumphed over death, and sorrow was turned into joy!

The dead youth was the widowed woman's only son. He had been the staff of her age, the comfort of her loneliness and the support of the home. The Bible records no loss so severe and painful as the loss of an only son. "When the Lord saw her, His quiet eyes singled out the grief stricken mother just behind the coffin." Under Jewish social life style, had this happened in Judea, the hired mourners and musicians would have preceded the bier. In Galilee, however, women who brought life into the world, ought to lead the death march of the funeral procession.

Our Lord's works of wonder spring not form the purpose of

offering His credentials of His mission, but from the outflow of
His infinite sympathy for human suffering. What a fullness of
compassion was compressed into the simple authoritative
summons, "Weep not."

Look! As Jesus touches the bier, or coffin, the procession
comes to a halt. Christ's compelling presence brought it to a
halt! Jesus did not fear the ceremonial defilement of contact
with the dead. Most Jewish rulers would have avoided touching the dead for fear of bringing on pollution! The people are
so quiet. Their sudden halt to the solemn march indicates awe,
respect and faith that the touch would be meaningful. Christ's
followers, who had witnessed many previous miracles, nevertheless were wonder-struck, as were the mourners, as they
thought, "What now!"

Jesus says, "Young man, I say unto thee, arise."

As soon as Christ's command, so effective in the kingdom of
death, was uttered, the dead youth sat up and spoke. Full vital-
ity was his as Christ raised him from the bier, as easily as
another from the bed.

Christ's power of resurrection proved Him to be God.
(Corinthians 1:9) Divinely commissioned prophets and apostles also became the media of resurrection, but with Christ it
was different. Everything was done in His name and in a direct
majestic manner. Power was not delegated to Him, all power
was His!

The spiritual application of this miracle is easy to see.
Having divine power to raise the physically dead, Christ is well
able, by virtue of His own approaching death and resurrection,
to raise to newness of life those who are dead in their sins and
trespasses. See how it all applies to us?

17. THE STILLING OF THE TEMPEST

(Luke 8:22–25; Matthew 8:23–27; Mark 4:35–41)

O
N THIS PARTICULAR DAY Jesus had been teaching His disciples when the crowd of people began to build up and throng Him. Jesus commanded His disciples to take Him in their boat to a quieter region of Peraea on the other side of the lake. It had been a most exhausting day of teaching and Jesus was weary and worn, both mentally and physically. Seeing how exhausted He was, the disciples made haste to get Him away for a brief repose and freedom from interruptions and distractions.

Throwing Himself upon the cushion, which was a standard part of the furnishings of a tiny craft, Jesus quickly fell fast asleep. Never did a ship carry a more precious cargo than this one. What a wonderful mingling of deity and humanity we see here in the boat. He, who never had need of sleep, has such a need now. So deep was His sleep that the sudden storm which distressed His disciples did not even disturb Jesus. To the fishermen the danger was very real and they were afraid for themselves and their divine Passenger. He, however, could sleep sweetly through the storm because He had perfect trust in His Heavenly Father's care and protection. This storm is really getting bad!

Undoubtedly the disciples abstained from disturbing Jesus for a while, but their need was desperate. So they aroused Him with the cry, "Lord, save us, lest we perish! Master, carest Thou not that we perish?"

He slept as the son of Man; but now as the Son of God, He awakes and rebukes the storm. His instrument of power is His word. He speaks, not loudly, and the wind ceases, and then there becomes a "great calm."

You and I are awestruck at the turn of events caused by God. He who was the co-creator of the winds and waves knows how to control them. When He became man, He did not lay aside His omnipotence. That is why in the sudden uproar on the lake, the forces of nature recognized His prerogative and yielded obedience to His word.

Turning from His rebuke of the storm, our Lord rebukes His disciples for their fearfulness and such little faith. "Why ye afraid? Where is your faith? Can any evil befall you while I am near?" The disciples were not absolutely faithless, for they had cried, "Master, save us!" It was only natural that they, as we, should be afraid, not just for their own safety, but for His. Just as in our case, yours and mine, when life's storms shake us, we simply have to step back, get control of ourselves, and ask God to still the waves of adversity. He will see us safely to shore. For a sinner rocked by the winds of sin and passion, there is hope if only he will cry, "Lord, save me or I will perish." Immediately He can and will bring peace to the storm-battered spirit!

18. THE TWO BLIND MEN

(Matthew 9:27–31)

BACK AT PETER'S HOUSE, another miracle occurred and was the literal fulfillment of the prophetic word relating to the ministry of the Messiah, "The eyes of the blind shall be opened." Those two men there followed Peter, hoping to be led to Jesus. They had heard of Jesus' supernatural healing power. By their ears they knew they had come near Jesus and they cried out, "Thou Son of David," indicating thereby the popular belief that Jesus was the expected Messiah as promised by the prophets of the Old Testament.

Their request for mercy and restoration of sight has been heard by Jesus, and He asked, "Believe ye that I am able to do this?" They replied, "Yes, Lord." By that reply Jesus knew they had faith in Him and He gave them their sight. Just like that, He made them able to see! Have you noticed that every incident of healing had to be preceded by faith? "According to your faith be it unto you."

Having confessed their faith, Jesus, by touching their eyes, immediately and generously honored that faith with the wonderful gift of sight. Look, in gloriously happy amazement they behold their Lord with their own eyes. Isn't that something to see? Looking into His caring blue eyes, and seeing that handsome face enclosed in light brown hair, they saw their Lord at last. The only known description of Jesus' appearance was found in a letter that a Roman official wrote back to his emperor in Rome. He had been stationed in Jerusalem as governor and had seen Jesus.

Jesus imposed silence upon the healing of the two blind men, telling them, "See that no man know it." But the men also could not keep it to themselves. The joyous men departed and spread Jesus' fame wherever they went. As you might imagine, they could not help but tell others of their miraculous cure.

Here is a copy of the report that Publius Lentulus wrote.

There lives, at this time, in Judea, a man of singular virtue whose name is Jesus Christ, whom the barbarians esteem as a prophet, but his followers love and adore him as the offspring of the immortal God. He calls back the dead from the graves, and heals all sorts of diseases with a word or a touch.

He is a tall man, and well shaped, of an amiable and reverend aspect; his hair of a color that can hardly be matched, the color of chestnut full ripe, falling in waves about his shoulders. His forehead high, large and imposing; his cheeks without spot or wrinkle, beautiful with a lovely red; his nose and mouth formed with exquisite symmetry; his beard thick and of a color suitable to his hair reaching below his chin. His eyes bright blue, clear and serene, look innocent, dignified, manly, and mature. In proportion of body, most perfect and captivating, his hands and arms most delectable to behold.

He rebukes with majesty, counsels with mildness, his whole address, whether in word or deed, being eloquent and grave. No man has seen him laugh, yet his manner exceedingly pleasant; but he has wept in the presence of men. He is temperate, modest and wise; a man, for his extraordinary beauty and divine perfections, surpassing the children of men in every sense.

Jesus and His disciples were real, honest-to-goodness, flesh-and-blood, breathing, eating men, as well as spiritual giants. Their divinity was expressed through their humanity. In fact, if Jesus were not man, there is little hope that any of us could follow Him—and he never seemed to have any doubt that we can follow Him.

19. The Dumb Demoniac

(Matthew 9:32–35)

THROUGH THE CROWD A deaf and dumb man is brought forward to Jesus by some of his friends. You see, knowledge of Jesus' power to heal was becoming very widespread. This man's condition was not the result of any local physical injury, neither was it congenital. Jesus knew, of course, that the man was possessed by a demon. Well, Jesus simply cast out the demon, and the man spoke as he was restored to sanity. He spoke words of praise to his Healer.

The multitudes who watched this miracle, as we did, "...marveled," saying, "It was never so seen in Israel." Beholding the cured man, they talked and gave free expression to their natural wonder and saw in Jesus their predicted Deliverer. Jesus wrought many, many miracles which attracted an ever increasing number of spectators. But that which impressed the people only further exasperated His enemies, who said, "He casteth out demons through the prince of demons." The name "Beelzebub" was considered to be the prince of demons. Jesus' enemies could not deny the reality of the miracles. As Israeli teachers and religious leaders, they professed their ability to cast out evil spirits, but a deaf and dumb man "possessed" was beyond their comprehension or reach of influence. But, they couldn't help but believe what we all saw.

20. THE GADARENE DEMONIAC

(Luke 8:26,27; Matthew 8:28–34; Mark 5:1–20)

JESUS' VISIT TO THE Gadarenes, or Gergasines, southeast across the Lake of Galilee, is only one incident, but what a striking incident it was! You will see what I mean. Jesus had only been in Gadara only a few hours when He found a demoniac and left behind a striking trophy of His power as a messenger to the people. This demon possessed man had the manifold personality of the one untamable wilderness inhabitant, guilty of self-mutilation with stones, naked and unclean, having immense muscular strength, and shrieking. Yet, he regained sanity and normalcy when delivered from demonic mastery through Jesus' pervasive power.

The presence of demon possession in the gospels is explained by attributing it to Babylonian and Persian beliefs or superstitions that had become part of Israeli beliefs. They applied physical and mental disorders to those displaying weird personality traits. Jesus assumed the role of corrector of these popular beliefs by commanding the supposed spirits to come out of the man. However, the clear unmistakable teaching of the Bible is that the Devil and evil spirits are real things, and that the Devil's power is exercised in a threefold manner, i.e., by himself, or by demons who are subject to his direction, and through human beings he has influenced, infiltrated, and possessed. Furthermore, scriptures offer abundant evidence of the reality of demons, such as former angelic beings who rebelled with Satan and who were expelled from Heaven with their master. Man's subjection to this power is the fruit of that fall and is a terrible reality not to be underrated.

This demonic man lived right here in this cemetery among the tombs. The man was naked, and lived in a sinful, shameless state. When he was bound with chains and fetters, his super-human strength enabled him to quickly break loose. "No man could bind him...no man could tame him!" He was also exceedingly fierce! But, when the demoniac saw Jesus from afar, he ran and worshipped Him. What a sight that was! Demons always recognized Jesus as the Lord and trembled and cringed before Him. The demoniac knew that Christ was no ordinary man who had dared to set foot in his desolate domain. Conscious of the vast gulf that divided them, and in his degraded condition, he realized he could have nothing to do with Jesus.

He yells to Jesus, "Thou Son of the most high God!" Although he feared torment before his time, Christ instead just commanded the unclean to come out of the man. However, the command is not immediately obeyed. The demon possessing the command was remonstrated, being unwilling to abandon his prey.

Jesus just asked the man, "What is your name?"

Whether it was the demon who answered, or the demon making the man reply, is not known. "My name is Legion, for we are many."

Furthermore, the demons presented a strange request of Jesus by asking to be allowed to enter a herd of swine nearby, a herd of about two thousand. "Go!" Jesus says. What glorious omnipotence was packed into that two-lettered command! Christ did not "send" the demons into the swine. "He merely drove them out of the man; all beyond that was merely per-missive."

Watch this! The swine, panic-stricken as they became demon-possessed, lose control of themselves on the steep decline and, once on the move, cannot stop! They run into the sea and all are drowned. Well, the watching Gadarenes saw what happened to their swine and ran to Jesus with fatal short-sightedness, and fear of such supernatural action. They demanded that Jesus depart from their coasts. The people were still afraid of the restored demoniac. They had never prayed before, but now they began "to pray that Jesus would depart."

Look at that! How graphic is the description of the delivered demoniac "sitting at the feet of Jesus, clothed and in his right mind!" He wanted to remain with Jesus as a disciple. Can you imagine that? What a clinging attitude of faith that is! Christ-possessed instead of demon-possessed.

The delivered man followed Jesus to the boat after Jesus was told to leave, and he prayed that he might accompany Christ. But Jesus saw that such was not the best discipline necessary for the man's spiritual growth. There was a better course of action for being a good disciple, namely, that of proclaiming to his own people and neighbors what Jesus had done for him. We can imagine what a stirring evangelist he must have become to those people around Gadara and Decapolis.

21. Jairus' Daughter

(Matthew 9:18–26; Mark 5:22–43; Luke 8:41–46)

Back on the west side of the lake, Jesus and the twelve disciples received a warm welcome upon their return to Capernaum. The word had traveled fast about the healing of the demoniac. The crowd gathered around the Master. One distressed man bowed before Jesus and presented a heartfelt plea for his dying daughter. See, Jesus listens and then immediately leaves for the man's house. On His way, however, He is briefly interrupted by a woman with an issue of blood. He quickly heals her and then continues on His way.

Jairus was one of the rulers, or princes, of the synagogue in Capernaum. Evidently the man knows much about the remarkable teachings of Jesus and because of His miraculous ministry he is convinced of His power. He sought the gift of healing for his beloved daughter. This ruler's reverent approach is a tribute to the honor in which Jesus was held by some of the Israeli religious leaders. Let's go along with them.

The little girl was about twelve years of age and the only child. Matthew wrote that she had just died. Christ never failed to respond to need. Unfailing readiness was His mission to the afflicted. Jesus turns to the bereaved father and says, "Fear not, believe only, and she shall be made whole." Christ gives hope to the father with His usual tenderness and compassion. He consoles the father. To the family and to us and the other mourners there, He says, "Weep not, she is not dead, but sleepeth." Then Christ asks that all of us leave the room, all except the parents. Present also are three of Jesus' disciples, Peter, James and John. These three are often selected from the others to be with Christ.

There in the quiet atmosphere of faith, the mighty work is accomplished. Jesus takes the frail corpse by the hand and says, "Maid, arise."

The Lord speaks only a brief word and the little girl springs to life! Then in thoughtfulness, Jesus says, "Give her meat." He was mindful and thoughtful over every need. His direction for nourishment indicated a weakened body which had to be strengthened with that restored life. He also charges the astonished parents that they should tell no man what had taken place. Now look at this resurrection miracle like this. Doesn't it predict the future in which there will be no more separation, when Christ will give us back our "unforgotten dearest dead," if they and we alike belong to Him?

22. FEEDING OF THE FIVE THOUSAND

(Matthew 14:13–21; Mark 6:31–44; Luke 9:10–17; John 6:1–14)

WATCH THIS MIRACLE JESUS, the omnipotent one, performs closely and observer because it is astounding. The importance of this event can be seen from the fact that it is mentioned by all four gospels written by those who were there, Matthew, Mark, Luke and John. Jesus' Lordship over nature and providence is clearly shown. He is concerned about bodily needs, as well as spiritual, and stands before us as the all-sufficient One. The pressure of circumstance over the death of John the Baptist, and the approaching of His own death in the following year, made it advisable to retire privately for rest, not just for Himself but also for His disciples who had returned from their first mission together. With them also were the disciples of John the Baptist who had brought the sad news of his murder. All of them needed a time of bodily and spiritual rejuvenation.

This miracle is exemplary also because of its magnitude. Christ's period of quietude was short-lived. The crowd of people continued to grow and to search Him out. When He and the disciples had reached the north end of Lake Galilee by boat, He found a multitude already here with us to greet Him. Nevertheless, He is obviously moved by compassion and He embraces the opportunity to teach them in one group and for healing the sick.

As the day wears on the disciples mention to Jesus that it is past lunchtime and the people are hungry. We didn't think to bring any food either. They thought that someone should be sent to seek the required food in the nearest town. But Jesus would not agree to that. He knew what He would do. Philip told Him they only had two hundred pennyworth of bread, and what could thirty-five dollars worth of bread do among the thousands of people.

Jesus could see no reason for the crowd to be send away, as He told Philip, "They need not depart." Knowing what He could do, Jesus was the personification of calmness. He said, "Give ye them to eat." One disciple said, "Shall we go and buy two pennyworth of bread to give them to eat?" Ignoring what was said, Jesus asks, "How many loaves have you? Go and see." Andrew stepped forward with the information that there was a lad there who had "five loaves and two small fishes." On hand, however, was the God who gave manna to the traveling Israelites, and He said, "I will satisfy the poor with bread." (Exodus 16, Psalm 132:15)

The lad gave the food, having no idea of the great possibilities of such a small amount. The food he had was prepared by his mother for him and his father to last the entire day. The loaves were of "barley," the food of the very poor, and the small fishes were a sort of salted sardine. The command was given for the people to sit down by companies on the grass. The spring season made the grass an attractive resting place on the green tableland.

To do things properly the orderly Jesus commanded the people to sit in groups of hundreds and fifties, proving that "order" is Heaven's first law. The crowd sat circle-like around Jesus, expectant and hungry. The 5,000 men sat around in the order indicated, and only the males were counted. How many women and children there were, we do not know. Their number, however, must have been considerable. Would you look at that crowd! There must be about 8,000 total!

How dramatic it was for Jesus to take the five loaves and two fishes in His hands and divide them, over and over again and give to the disciples to distribute. The people sat there in hushed expectancy. Before the food is handed out to the people by the disciples, Jesus gives thanks to God, an exquisite instance of grace before eating. Watch that! Making five loaves of bread and two fishes feed that many people is certainly the interposition of God.

Just as Jesus blessed the meal, He broke bread. Since Jewish loaves are thin, a thumb's breath in thickness, they are more easily broken than cut. The duplication of food affords example and proof of Christ's deity. The miracle this day is done by Christ's own hands and mediated to the multitude by human hands, for He gives the blessed and miracle-produced loaves to His disciples who in turn distribute them to the people. Because the food is served by the disciples, the people ate more hardily as it seemed more friendly, and the disciples were enshrouded by Christ's spirit by sharing in His work.

Look, there is certainly nothing skimpy about the Lord's provision. After all the people have been adequately fed, the disciples collect what is left of the bread and fishes. Look at that! Twelve baskets! Jesus sees to it that there is no food wasted. A large bounty and the precise economy go hand-in-hand. The people are free to take what they want when they head for home.

What about the lad's reward for not withholding what he had, but surrendering it for the Master's use? Well, what a thrill he must have experienced as he watched Jesus miraculously multiply the little he gave. Christ gave him good measure, for he is taking home a glad heart and enough food for his whole family.

The enthusiasm created by this miracle is intense. The young lad could hardly believe what he was seeing, and neither could we, except for the fact that we saw it with our heart's eye. The people wanted to enthrone Jesus as King immediately and have Him lead them in a triumphant march to Jerusalem for the Passover celebration. In their outburst of enthusiasm the people felt that a mighty ruler would indeed be a boon to long over-taxed people! But Jesus refused the Kingdom offer. He knew the kingdom would eventually be His, not by man's hand, but by God's.

The lesson we receive from this great miracle is that Christ is truly the bread of life to a perishing world. Those in their sin and indifference need not depart. Christ gave through the disciples. He waits to offer others the knowledge and experience of His all-sufficiency.

23. WALKING ON THE WATER

(Matthew 14:22–36; Mark 6:45–54; John 6:15–21)

THAT EVENING AFTER JESUS had fed the 5,000 plus, He constrained His disciples to set out in the boat for the western shore of the Sea of Chinnereth. They didn't want to go without Him, but went along with what He wanted. To them no day had ever been so bright!

As for Jesus, after the frenzy of the people wanting to make Him King, He just wanted to return to the mountain for rest, solace, and communion with God, so he went walking by himself.

Later, on the lake, on the way back toward Capernaum, the disciples became hard put, because one of the sudden furious storms common to the area gave the strong rowers hours of useless toil. Three hours after midnight they had only gone halfway across the lake. They were tossed and tormented by the waves, for the winds were "contrary." What the weary rowers did not know was that Jesus, in His solitude, was cognizant of their plight. The disciples were shortly to learn of the Master's divine sympathy and His willingness to enter into the struggle. Thus it was that Jesus went to them in a most unexpected way, by walking on the water, as if it were a soft, smooth carpet. Every new experience of Jesus was an awe-filled surprise to the disciples. They were almost exhausted when, suddenly, they saw an apparition through the dark night and they shouted, "It's a spirit!" But they were soon to know that which seemed to be a specter, was nothing else but their Savior!

Behold the infinite ease Jesus moves naturally and majestically over the troubled waters. He sought to calm those in the boat with a cheering call, "It is the great 'I Am'! Be not afraid!" How reassuring His voice must have been then. "The majesty of His approach was perfected in the tenderness of the address." Immediately our fears were calmed!

At the heart of the miracle was Jesus' walking on the sea. We must consider the direct affront to the law of nature. Is there a logical explanation? No, there was no suspension of the accepted universal law of gravity, but rather just the exercise of a stronger supernatural power! This was the exercise of Christ's omnipotence, as He, the Creator of seas and winds, revealed His authority over them. It is difficult for us finite humans to believe, even when we see it happen!

Yes, when man contemplates the works and ways of God, the question always arises, "How can these things happen?" Such a question, however, is simply of unbelief. Actually, no miracle should stagger the heart that has learned to trust in God and to believe in His Word. With Him all things are possible. Convinced that it was indeed the Christ, the lovable, impetuous Peter, the spokesman of the apostolic group, said, "Lord, if it be Thou, bid me to come unto Thee on the water." Jesus replied, "Come." Peter steps onto the waters and, at first, his faith sustained him and he takes a few steps on the water. He shared with his Master the "greatness of Spiritual life which overrides the action of natural laws by the One who is supernatural."

Although the faith of Peter was not a pure courageous faith, but a human over-boldness, it was sufficient to enable the "attempt." Looking at the huge nearby waves, Peter suddenly becomes afraid and cries out, "Lord, save me!" The delegated power of faith had left him and, although a strong swimmer, the waters began to engulf him. As he began to sink, Jesus saves him simply by taking his hand and raising him up to the edge of the boat. With Peter, Jesus boarded the boat and, immediately, the winds ceased. What an amazing event.

Once Jesus was settled in the craft and all was calm, the disciples had a fresh look of His Greatness. They openly worshipped Him, saying, "Of a truth Thou art the Son of God." This is always the attitude of those of us delivered by Christ's power.

Don't you see that, in this case, the lesson of this miracle is both instructive and comforting? Faith is tested by the storms of life, but God is always near. When tossed to and fro on the waves of the world, it may sometimes seem that He has forgotten us, but not so. He comes to help us in marvelous ways. When the storms of this life confront us and we begin to sink into dismay and doubt, may our cry be, "Lord, save me!" And He will do it.

24. The Syro-Phoenician Woman's Daughter

(Matthew 15:21–28; Mark 7:24–30)

THE INCIDENT THAT WE now see is happening only a few days after the feeding of the five thousand. Jesus' labors, henceforth, consist of a succession of tours and journeys and unrecorded miracles. Peril increased because king Herod was very suspicious and the Pharisees could not conceal their hostility and hatred toward Him. Feeling the need for seclusion and the need for further disciple instruction, Jesus sought the seclusion of a friend's home and wanted no one to know about it. His concealment turned out to be short, for the more He tried to hide, the more He became known and sought. So great a physician cannot go unnoticed in a world of suffering.

Jesus' escape was northwest toward the borders of Tyre and Sidon. A woman from that heathen area—a pagan outside the Covenant—was to refresh His distressed spirit through a single deed of mercy. This miracle revolves around the Syro-Phoenician's race, religion, reason, reception and reward. The woman who came to Jesus lived in Phoenicia which was then regarded as part of Syria. She was a Greek, which meant "Gentile." As a Phoenician, she worshipped the great mother goddess, "Ashtoreth," or "Astarte," or "Queen of heaven," giver of life. It was a belief in plant, animal, and man. This so-called goddess was supposed to give to her devotees everything evil. Yes, and this was a woman from that country stained with infamy and sin, coming to Jesus, conscious of her own personal shortcomings, seeking divine mercy for herself and her demon-possessed daughter.

She was a pagan and, personally, the only known example of a heathen being blessed by our Lord. Another Gentile, you remember, the Capernaum centurion, was also helped by Jesus, but it was already obvious that he was a convert to the Jewish faith. This woman's daughter was "grievously vexed with a devil" (demon), and was the reason the woman approached Jesus. One of the devil's fallen spirits had entered and taken possession of the girl, resulting in total disability. Of course, her mother was unable to do anything for her relief. She now appeals to Jesus, "Have mercy on me, O Lord, Thou Son of David, my daughter is grievously vexed with a devil."

Probably this distressed mother was a widow, and therefore all the more anxious to get help for her child. She addressed Jesus as Lord, which reveals her respect for Him. She, like most people, had heard much about His reputation. But, surprisingly, here she receives a seemingly chilly reception as Jesus "answered her not a word." Because of His omniscience, He knew all about the woman and why she had come to Him. Look, Jesus just gets up and leaves the house. But she is not to be put off, for she follows Him with her entreaties, so much so that the disciples are annoyed and appeal to Jesus, "Send her away"—give her what she wants, in other words, and dismiss her. It was thought, "He delays the answer with a divine 'much more' of mercy and grace in which He means to bless her." To the disciples He says, "I am not sent but unto the lost sheep of the house of Israel."

What happens next is most impressive. Watch. Overhearing what was said to His disciples about His exclusive ministry, the woman comes close and worships Him, saying, "Lord, help me." With the renewal of her passionate entreaty, Jesus pauses. Up to now He had spoken to His disciples, now He speaks to the woman in words meaning, "You are not of Israel to whom I am sent. It is the children's bread I have come to give, and you are outside the family circle." The woman, however, is not discouraged by Christ's words. With perfect logic she draws the sweetest meaning out of their seeming bitterness. This woman's faith is so strong that she turns the repulse of Jesus into a reason for approaching Him again, changing dissuasion into persuasion. "True, Lord; yet the dogs eat of the crumbs which fall from their master's tables." Accepting His point of view, she admitted that she was a Gentile and therefore should be called a "dog," but as such should not be excluded from having some food, but rather should receive some of it.

Jesus had tried her faith by His silence and by His discouraging replies, that He might see the strength of it. He turns to her and says, "O woman, great is thy faith, be it unto thee even as thou wilt." Her unparalleled faith in Christ proved that it is not blood, proving the true Abraham lineage, but faith, and tried by that test, she is a spiritual daughter of Abraham.

The patient was not in sight of the Healer when she was cured. The woman believed that nearness or distance made no difference to His power to heal her daughter, and so she went home in perfect confidence, there to find her loved one healed. The mother went forth unto her people as a missionary and the Church at Tyre grew to large proportions thereafter.

25. THE DEAF AND DUMB MAN OF DECAPOLIS

(Mark 7:31–37)

A<small>FTER</small> J<small>ESUS</small>' <small>SPECIAL JOURNEY</small> to the borders of Tyre and Sidon, and the healing of the Syro-Phoenician's daughter, He made a circuit of the Decapolis district. It is an area encompassing ten cities which had been given special privileges by the Roman conquerors about a century earlier. Here, as everywhere else, Jesus and His disciples found need for His divine might and mercy. Multitudes came bringing their lame and sick to be healed, and He did just that.

Of all those who were healed, Mark had selected one sufferer because of the unusual incidents associated with the need. The man was not completely a deaf-mute. Although deaf, he could mutter some words through a severe speech impediment. However, after Christ's touch, he was able to speak plainly. The tongue of a dumb person was considered in ancient popular belief to have been bound by a demon. But in this case, demonic impediment was not mentioned as being the cause. The tongue of the unsaved man is as estranged from God as his ear. Even the most cultured sinner betrays an impediment in his speech whenever spiritual truths are mentioned.

The methods Jesus used for healing this "deaf stammerer" were unique. There was nothing stereotyped, anyway, about His methods. In this case, as we see, they were not so much means by which He conveyed healing, but were signs intended to explain to the sufferer's mind how healing was to come. Because of His wisdom and omnipotence, Jesus works in ways He deems best.

Look, Jesus takes the man aside from the crowd. Without interruption, Jesus wants to awaken in the man a more confident hope, with an assured faith that he is going to be healed. We understand the need to get away briefly from the noise of the multitude. It is in the hush of God's presence that we learn of our sin and guilt and our deep need for sovereign grace.

Isolating the man from the crowd, the first thing Jesus does is to put His fingers to the ears of the deaf man. Since he could not hear, it had to be by touch that he would be most encouraged. The man did not speak plainly, because he could not hear, therefore that defect was the first removed. Then with His own spittle on His finger, He touches the man's tongue. Next, Jesus is written of as "looking up to heaven," and that upward look is a sign to the deaf man whence cometh His power. Such a heavenward look is also an acknowledgment of His Oneness with the Father. With His glance there is also a groan, for "He sighed." The scene sets before us the solitary Savior in the presence of sin and sufferings of a lost race, and how His deep sympathy springs from His lofty communion with God. Immediately the man can hear and speak distinctly. The entire process of establishing communication between the centers of hearing and of speech is bridged in a moment. In the spiritual realm it is the same, for the ear must be opened to receive divine instruction before the tongue is able to speak forth God's praise.

As to the result of this miracle, Jesus charged those who witnessed it to tell no man. Jesus desires no cheap popularity. But, as always, the more He asked that they be quiet about it, the more they spread abroad the publicity. Many of those in the heathen regions of Decapolis witnessing the work of Jesus, confessed that He had chosen Israel for His own possession and was God above all.

26. FEEDING OF THE FOUR THOUSAND

(Matthew 15:30–38; Mark:1–9)

THIS "DOUBLE MIRACLE," SIMILAR to the miracle of the feeding of the five thousand, actually takes place not very far from that one, but the occasion and motive in the two miracles are different. The 5,000 were fed at the head of the lake, where the River Jordan flows into it and in the district of Bethesda. The 4,000 are fed on the northeastern shore of the lake in the general region of Tyre and Sidon. In this case, Jesus is with the multitude for three days at this event only seven weeks after the other feeding. There are 4,000 men, plus approximately 2,300 women and children, or a total of 6,300.

A great number of Gentiles had followed Jesus from the region of Decapolis, and attracted by His marvelous teaching, remained with Him also for three days. On the third day, Jesus, proposing to send the people back to their homes, is concerned about the shortage of food for their physical comfort. Any food they had brought with them was virtually all gone, and they needed some to sustain them on their way home. Jesus knew that He must act. He says to His disciples, "I have compassion on the multitude, because they continue with Me now three days, and have nothing to eat; and I will not send them away fasting, lest they faint by the way." What a revelation this is of divine compassion and consideration!

Jesus asked how much food was on hand, and the disciples replied, "Seven loaves, and a few little fishes." That was not even enough for one meal for the twelve disciples. Jesus knew what He would do. He commands the multitude to be seated in orderly fashion and then gives thanks. They are all served from Jesus' hand by the disciples. When the meal is finished and all are satisfied, Jesus sends them on their way. He does not leave first. As host, Jesus waits until His guests have gone with a benediction. Then He and His disciples board ship and go over to the coast of Magdala.

Here again we have seen that Jesus is "the bread of life for hungry hearts." Spiritually, we have nothing of ourselves which can quicken and support our souls, but in Christ there is true sustenance which all can appropriate by faith.

27. THE BETHESDA BLIND MAN

(Mark 8:22–26)

HERE IN BETHESDA THIS miracle also happens near the place where the five thousand were fed. The friends of a blind man brought him from his home to gain contact with the great Healer. They apparently thought it was necessary for Jesus to touch him in order to restore his sight. But Jesus dealt with individuals usually, individually and personally, and not in a methodical way.

The first step is the applying of spittle moisture from the Lord's mouth to the eyes of the blind man. He used that which was of His physical Self. Christ's variety of healing methods proves that He is not bound by any particular method. As the omnipotent One, He can heal with or without means, because He, Himself, was and is the true source of healing and of life. Listen, Christ's question of the man is, "Dost thou see ought?" The man raises his head and says, "I see men as trees walking." This ability to describe what he sees shows that he had not been born blind. Although he knew they were men, he could not discern the shapes in any detail. Touching the man's eyes again, Jesus bade him to look up, and this time full and complete vision is his! Sight is no longer blurred and indistinct! Eye surgeons of our day know what it is to heal defective sight by degrees. At first, a glimmer of light is allowed, for the optic nerve must grow accumstomed to the light before the eyeballs can stand the full light of day. The first person he sees is Jesus! What a beautiful way to awaken to eyesight! Jesus tells the man that he should go home, avoiding town on his way so as not to publicize the miracle. Whether the man respected the request any better than the others we have seen and heard about, we do not know. We can have the glory of spiritual vision and be brought out of the darkness into His most marvelous light just by believing in Him. Our daily prayer should be that the Spirit might open our eyes of understanding to discern more fully the divine will of God in our life. Amen.

28. THE TRANSFIGURATION

(Matthew 17:1–13; Mark 1:11–13; Luke 1:16–18)

THIS REMARKABLE INTERLUDE IN the life of our Lord is record-ed in much the same language as in the first three gospels, Matthew, Mark and Luke, and all represent it as taking place about six to eight days after His distinct announcement of His approaching death and resurrection. What happened on the Mount of Transfiguration, that mountain over there, west of Damascus, occurred shortly before Christ's final departure from Galilee and between four to six days before His death.

Everything about that night on the "Holy Mount" when Jesus went up on Mount Hermon to pray was simply dazzling! He took three of His disciples with Him. By choosing John, Peter, and James, Jesus confirmed these three as primates among the twelve so that they might have faith in His foretold sufferings. Such a glorious experience was intended to confirm their faith in Christ's divine glory and to prepare them for dark days ahead, which were already overshadowing His actions. The three are completely dazzled by a blinding light; the Heavenly radiance of Christ is manifest! Look at that, if you can!!! Jesus' face shines like the sun! Through full communion with His Father, divine glory flows out into visible brightness! As we see, not only is there a change in His outward appear-

ance, but there is an outflashing of His inner nature, essentially divine! Deity shows through the glorified face and shining
raiment! That radiance is the revelation of His Incarnate Deity.

Jesus' evident glory manifestation also suffused His gar-
ments, changing them into dazzling brightness! They are "as
bright as the light!" There, appearing in glorified form, yes, it is
Moses and Elijah! The two Old Testament saints are appearing
before Jesus, the Christ. They are talking! The theme of their
conversation has to do with "Calvary." Peter had previously
urged Jesus not to speak of His death, but Moses and Elijah
came all the way from Heaven to talk about nothing else.
Amazing! These two saints were chosen by God from among
the myriads of saints in Heaven to come to this Mount and do
Homage to the Son of God! Well, Moses was the greatest representative of the Law, which he brought from God to Israel
from another Mount. Under that Law the people were to live
from the time of Moses to the time of Christ. Elijah was the
suitable representative of the Godly fellowship of the prophets
and of their statements of prophecy. Moses and Elijah
appeared to witness the passing of the Old Order, and to hail
the coming of the "New Testament" and the New Covenant
provisions of Salvation. Yes, in Christ there has come a transfiguration of character and life, of outlook and hope for the
peoples of the World.

29. THE DEMONIC BOY

(Matthew 17:14–21; Mark 9:14–29; Luke 9:37–43)

FROM MOUNT HERMON JESUS descended from the harmony of fellowship with Moses and Elijah into some of the wildest and harshest discords on Earth. From the Father's honor and Glory, He now comes to face the hatred and murderous intents of the religious leaders who are thirsting for His blood.

As Jesus walks along, a distressed father approaches Him with true humility and reverence. "He kneeled down to Him." As one of a multitude of people, he comes forward to make a plea on behalf of the miserable case of his only child. What heartache must have been his! Love for, and anguish over, his lunatic boy made him bold. He first asks for help of the disciples, but they felt unable to do anything. The disciples became depressed over their failure to cure, or even to attempt a cure, for the boy. They should have been able to cure had they but made use of the Savior's name. The nine found themselves baffled. This new challenge perplexed them, and they were humiliated before the onlookers, especially the scribes who were watching. They were looking for a chance to sneer.

Christ says, "Bring him hither to me." The boy's terrible symptoms are severe convulsions, foaming at the mouth, grinding his teeth, and rigidity of the body. And because of unexpected attacks, he often fell into the fire or into the water. The word "lunatic" was used to describe such a condition and meant "moonstruck;" luna being the latin word for "moon." Epilepsy, from which the boy suffered, was supposed to have been inflicted on persons who had sinned against the "moon." Because the fits were sudden and long lasting, it was phrased "that the devil hardly departed from him."

No case, however, is too different for Christ, to whom all power is given. After rebuking the faithless crowd, both scribes and disciples, Jesus rebukes the devil, or demon, possessing the boy, who immediately departs out of him and the boy is cured! Jesus says to the demon, "I charge thee, enter no more into him." Look there at the poor father. He has witnessed so many relapses that Christ's complete and permanent cure has thrilled his heart. Taking the boy's hand, Jesus raises him up and delivers him to his father's arms. Christ's healing grace has been seen by all of us with delight. Now, calmness, peace and self-possession are seen instead of the convulsive agony. Here the spiritual of the Healer has overcome the force, whether morbid or demonic, that was the cause of the boy's suffering.

Isn't it wonderful and reassuring to see and to know that there is no impotence in Christ, and that every woe of the human heart yields to His control. Demons and humans recognize His way.

30. The Man Born Blind

(John 9:1–41)

W E, AND A BUNCH of people, are walking along a road following Jesus. This road surely is dusty and dry. It's no wonder that much foot washing is customary when people go into a house. The sandals that are worn, like those that Jesus is wearing permit dusty and dirty feet. We are all watching Jesus, glorifying in his presence, and our eyes are filled with admiration. What a stately figure, and what soft, beautiful eyes He has. You could even say that His eyes are heavenly blue.

I know of no other descriptions of Jesus except that written by the Governor of Judea, Publius Lentulus in a letter addressed to Tiberius Caesar, then Emperor of Rome. He had seen Jesus many times and described Him as follows.

"There lives, at this time, in Judea, a man of singular virtue whose name is Jesus Christ, whom the barbarians esteem as a prophet, but his followers love and adore him as the offspring of the immortal God. He calls back the dead from the graves, and heals all sorts of diseases with a word or a touch.

He is a tall man, and well-shaped, or an amiable and reverend aspect; his hair of a color that can hardly be matched, the color of a chestnut full ripe, falling in waves about his shoulders. His forehead high, large and imposing; his cheeks without spot or wrinkle, beautiful with a lovely red; his nose and mouth formed with exquisite symmetry; his beard thick and of a color suitable to his hair reaching below his chin. His eyes, bright blue, clear and serene, look innocent, dignified, manly, and mature. In proportion of body, most perfect and captivating, his hands and arms most delectable to behold.

He rebukes with majesty, counsels with mildness, his whole address, whether in word or deed, being eloquent and grave. No man has seen him laugh, yet his manner is exceedingly pleasant; but he has wept in the presence of men. He is temperate, modest, and wise; a man, for his extraordinary beauty and divine perfections, surpassing the children of men in every sense."

Governor Publius Lentulus was obviously impressed with Jesus, having seen Him and heard Him speak. Having walked with Him, you and I can see why the Governor was impressed with Jesus, as virtually anyone was who has walked with him.

Jesus and His disciples were real, honest-to-goodness, flesh-and-blood, breathing, eating men, as well as spiritual giants. Their divinity was expressed through their humanity. In fact, if Jesus were not man, there is little hope that any of us could follow Him—and He never seemed to have any doubt that we could follow Him.

What a blessing, that we are walking with Him now. Look, Jesus sees a blind beggar on the side of the road. He tarries to heal the man without any request on his part. This is a Sabbath day, and a Sabbath miracle irritates the Jewish leaders because of the distorted views about the Sabbath. Our Lord knows that. In spite of the murderous animosity of His enemies, Jesus is immortal until His work is finished. Jesus had said, "I must work the works of Him that sent Me." None could hurt Him or "penetrate with word or stone the encasing envelope of the presence of God. Secure in that protection, He was able to come and go, fearless and unharmed, serene and quiet, restful and peaceful, blessing and blessed." Yes, Jesus is beyond hurt, unless permitted, eventually, by God to serve the purpose of God.

The sight of the beggar and the knowledge that he had been

born blind prompted the question of the disciples, "Who did sin, this man, or his parents, that he was born blind?" It was common belief that afflictions were the result of sin and were the punishment for those sins. The fact that he was born blind excludes the possibility that his plight was caused by his sinning. It was common Jewish belief that the inequities of the parents would appear in their offspring. The answer of Jesus was explicit that, in this case, neither the man himself nor his parent's sinning had caused the man's blindness.

Jesus just spits on the ground and makes clay of the spittle. Such action was common by the physicians of that time in treating various maladies. Here the reason for placement of spittal-clay on the man's eyes is to evoke hope and expectation in him. The latent power of faith needed to be stirred, and the sufferer to be made conscious that it is Jesus who is the Healer. The Divine had lead the man to expect a cure, hence his prompt obedience to the Lord's command. Both the blind man and those of us standing around are made aware of the fact that the actual power of healing is in Jesus alone.

The command was for the man to arise and go wash his eyes in the pool of Siloam. Such a command is a still further test of the man's faith, to confirm and strengthen it. Healing results immediately; "he washed, and came seeing." Usually, in the recovery of sight, seeing needs to be slowly learned. But the "acquired perceptions of sight" are not necessary here. Jesus gives the man perfect sight so that he can see clearly as soon as he opens his eyes.

How commendable was the man's implicit faith, his fearless confession of his healing to his neighbors and to the hostile Pharisees; his utter disregard of consequences because of his previous expulsion from the synagogue, his brave confession, his belief in, and worship of, the Son of God! What a glorious conclusion to this miraculous event! He has experienced "new life" because of belief and faith in Jesus.

31. The Infirm Woman

(Luke 13:10–17)

THIS MIRACLE WAS OF special interest to Luke, the physician, gifted historian, and disciple who witnessed it but did not tell of the time or place. He simply tells us that it happened in one of the synagogues on a Sabbath day. You and I don't quite know where we are, but here we are in a synagogue leaning against a wall and watching. It's a fact that on no other day of the week is our Lord more closely watched by His adversaries as on the Sabbath, in the hope that they might trap Him in some breach of the "law." They don't know that their sin is heightened by the fact that they are supposed to be the religious leaders of God's chosen people. I wonder if, later, any of them come to believe in Jesus' Divinity.

The physical condition of the infirm woman is pitiable to the extreme. For eighteen years she has endured her deformity. At some time she had a mysterious derangement of the nervous system. Her physical curvature was the consequence and made an enduring melancholy. She was bowed at the waist and unable to straighten up. A dislocation of the vertebrae was indicated.

Her title as "a daughter of Abraham" suggests that she was one of the inner circle of pious Israelites. On this day the inheritress of Abraham is in the right place to be healed. Her crippled state could not keep her from the House of God.

The woman's condition appealed to the sensitive spirit of Jesus, so He calls to her and says, "Woman, thou art loosed from thine infirmity." She had not applied to Him for healing, but he did not wait to be asked. Her faithful devotion made her worthy and receptive to the healing power of Jesus. He lays His hand on her and she is immediately made straight. She stands now, straight and "glorified in God." Look at that! She is purring forth her joy in a continuous thanksgiving to the gracious Author of her cure which became a voluntary act of praise before all the people.

But the miracle has had a different effect on the ruler of the synagogue, and he is pouring out his anger upon Jesus! He just shouted that there are six other days in the week in which to work without profaning the Sabbath. Our Lord answers His adversary with such unusual severity as to shame the man into silence. "Thou hypocrite!" When God prescribed the Sabbath for man, forbidding him to work therein, except in emergencies, He did not thereby bind His own hands and make it improper for Himself to work, mercifully, on that day. Not any day can stay Him in His ministry of grace and power.

While His adversaries attacked Jesus verbally and then were ashamed, the other people around Him "rejoiced" for all the glorious things being done by Him.

32. THE MAN WITH DROPSY

(Luke 14:1–6)

C AN YOU BELIEVE THIS? The Pharisees invited Jesus to a
Sabbath feast! Do you suppose He was invited so that they
might charge Him with blasphemy? They certainly "watched"
Jesus to see what He might do next. They are sitting at the same
table with God incarnate, yet they are so blind that they know
Him not. Jesus accepted the invitation with love, even though
He knew it had not been offered in good faith. Their attitude
of "watching" was to discover an accusation to charge Him
with.

It was possibly planned that by bringing a dropsical man to
the feast, it might cause a confrontation with Jesus, because of
His propensity for the afflicted. Jesus knew that the infirm person himself had no part in a plot. Whether he was invited out
of respect, idle curiosity, or through craft, Jesus used the occasion to shame His foes.

"Jesus had no compunction or conscience about feasting on
such a day, but to heal the sick was unforgivable" *(Mark 3:1–6)*.
Sabbath feasts were an integral part of the social life of the
Jews. Plutarch, the Roman, said of the feasts, "The Hebrews
honor the Sabbath day chiefly by inviting each other to drink-
ing and intoxication." Though supposedly religious, the

Pharisees did not abstain from debauchery on the Sabbath, but rather turned it into a day of riot and drunken excess. Jesus accepted invitations to feasts with publicans and sinners knowing full well that the occasion would afford Him the platform for His grace and power.

The afflicted guest had the "dropsy," an organic disease, characterized by edema or swelling of various parts of the body from heart or kidney malfunction. Luke was there also and his medical training certainly influenced his writing style and language, both prevalent with technical phraseology.

Look. Without further hesitation Jesus walks up to the man, touches him, and the disease is gone. The cure was unasked for, but graciously given. The healed man is allowed to leave the feast joyously before Jesus resumed His conversation with His critics. Jesus asks the questions first, not the Pharisees, but they cannot answer Him, or else are powerless to answer Him. Here, if an animal had fallen into a pit on a Sabbath day, it is comparable to a man in danger of death from dropsy. But such a public silencing only further irritates the crowd and stiffens their antagonism toward Christ. By thus healing the dropsical man, Jesus proved that it is more merciful to heal a man on the Sabbath than to extricate an ox from a ditch. There, such reasoning shuts the mouths of those whose hearts were destitute of mercy towards suffering humanity.

This is the last of the seven recorded miracles having occurred on the Sabbath. As a day of public worship, Jesus honored it, especially as a day of showing mercy through healing. The Lord's Day is consecrated by His Spirit for the service of man, as well as for the worship of God. Christ lived to relieve the afflicted and oppressed. As we know, He later died to emancipate men and women from a worse disease than that of the body. Thank God, Jesus can take the person afflicted with the disease of sin, heal him and let that person go out to walk in the "newness" of living.

33. RAISING OF LAZARUS FROM THE GRAVE

(John 11:1–46)

IT WAS ABOUT A month before His own death and resurrection that Jesus went along this road to Bethany and wrought His third miracle of resurrection. Bethany is only about five miles from Jerusalem, just a stroll for Jesus. There it is ahead. The circumstances of this beautiful miracle speaks irresistibly for historical truth, and the objections or disbelief raised by critical writers and readers really centers in their own aversion to the miraculous. It was the most remarkable of all His mighty works, and foreshadowed His own resurrection and also made a profound impression in Jerusalem.

Jesus often visited this home of Mary, Martha, and Lazarus. It was a good place to be for Jesus where He was loved and understood and where His wounded spirit found rest. Their parents were dead and Lazarus and his two sisters comprised a delightful home circle. These three loved each other, and each one had faith in the despised and rejected Messiah. Each in turn was equally loved by Him.

We are not told the nature of Lazarus' sickness, but it was obviously serious because the sisters sent a friend to tell their

Healer to come to his aid. The information the sisters sent was expressed simply, "Lord, behold, he whom thou lovest is sick." When Jesus received the news—because of His omniscience He already knew about it. He said to the messenger and to His disciples that such sickness and its conclusion, were being permitted for two reasons. The first was the furtherance and accomplishment of the purpose and glory of God, and the second was that Jesus Himself might be glorified thereby. What must have been hard to understand was the delay of Jesus. He not only permitted the sickness, but allowed it to continue unto death. His delays were not denials. There are qualities which unrelieved suffering can perfect in any person. Jesus Himself "Learned obedience by the things that He suffered." Jesus remained where He was for two more days before starting toward Bethany.

Mary and Martha were confident that Jesus would come quickly, but you can see the anguish written on their faces. No wonder that when Jesus came up that road, the sisters, with minds so perplexed over His strange delay, ran to Him and said, "Lord, if Thou hadst been here my brother would not have died!" Jesus' sympathy is great, so much so that tears came into His eyes, not for the dead, but through sympathy for the beloved sisters. He wanted them to understand, and us, that whatever our power to help friends, or our inclination to do so, we must be guided in the exercise of that power by a regard for God's glory.

It is to be noted that before Jesus left for the sorrowing home in Bethany, He gave the disciples a beautiful description of death. He knew that Lazarus had died and He said, "Our friend Lazarus sleepeth; but I go, that I may awake him out of sleep." His disciples thought He was referring to natural sleep and that Lazarus, after a good sleep, would recover from his sickness. Then Jesus said plainly, "Lazarus is dead." You see, what sleeps is the body, not the spirit within the body. The spirit, absent from the body, but present with the Lord, is in a blissful, conscious state. The body will sleep in the dust, only awaiting resurrection.

When Jesus ultimately arrives, Lazarus has been in his tomb

for four days. Martha, glad to see Jesus, says to Him, "Lord, by this time he stinketh." Deterioration had begun, but a memorable miracle was about to be performed. The ravages of decay, through divine power, were stayed, and the natural processes were reversed.

It was Martha who confessed faith in His Messiahship, "Yes, Lord, I believe that Thou art the Christ, the Son of God, which could come into the world," and believing, she knew that He was able to recall her brother to life. How assuring the message must have been when Jesus said, "Thy brother shall arise again." With the sisters, as stated in the shortest verse in the Bible, "Jesus wept." His sympathy with human sorrow is not less a part of His nature than the union with divine strength. As Jesus walks toward the tomb His tears flowed, causing the bystanders to say, "Behold how He loved him." Now, what is He going to do?

In watching this miracle we see a valuable testimony to the humanity of Jesus' "human" emotions. How amazed we are at the miracle of His humanity. He loved, and He needed the comfort of a home. Jesus could be glad and smile, He had need of prayer, and He wept. Yet deity and humanity are combined in this miracle. As the man, Jesus wept. As god, He stopped and shouted, "Lazarus, come forth!" As the man, He sympathizes with us in our sorrows, and as the God on earth, He can banish them.

Jesus prays and praises God for the result He knows will happen. Then He turns to His disciples and says, "Take ye away the stone." That action did not call for a miracle. With the exercise of His will, He could have caused the stone to roll away, without saying a word. But Jesus never imposed His power for personal acclaim. He never performed a miracle unless it was necessary to glorify God. With the stone rolled away, look, Lazarus is coming out still wrapped in his burial linen!

"Loose him, and let him go," Jesus says.

The lesson apparent from this stupendous miracle is easy for us to see. Christ is the Quickener of the dead, spiritually and physically. His life-giving miracle of grace is as truly remarkable as His quickening miracle of power. At the appointed hour He will raise all persons redeemed by His blood to glory with Himself in the Father's home, and, in the final dissolution of all things, He will raise all His foes for their fateful resurrection and for their final "judgment" before God.

34. THE TEN LEPERS

(Luke 17:11–19)

O N HIS LAST PILGRIMAGE to Jerusalem, Jesus passes through Samaria and Galilee, areas He knew so well and in which the people had witnessed His power and many believed in Him. Usually, when the Jews went to Jerusalem they took the longer route across Jordan in order to avoid the inhospitable Samaritans with whom the Jews had no dealings. Jesus, however, does not acknowledge petty differences between people, as He came as the Savior of all people who will believe in Him. Look, if you can, at that miserable group of lepers bound together in their affliction. Only one of them is a Samaritan, the others are Jews. Together they form a grotesque group, with disheveled hair, torn and dirty clothes, and with bowed heads. A cloth covers their heads except for the upper part of their faces. Jesus sees them huddled together off to one side of the road and He has sympathy for them you can tell by the expression on His face.

They had heard about Jesus. From the depth of their misery they cried out to the Healer, "Lord, have mercy on us!" Jesus looks at them. The attitude of His compassion is so impressive. He simply says to them, "Go shew yourselves to the priests." They probably thought, "Well, why not. We will try anything," and as they depart, they are healed! Can you imagine the cry of joy coming from one and then another as they saw in each other the wonderful transformation! You know they must have felt the flood of new life wash through those wasted frames. They had enough faith to do what they were told, but they weren't healed until their faith grew stronger.

By telling them to go to the priests, Jesus showed that He had not come to break the law, but to fulfill it. Here it seems that Jesus varied His treatment procedure according to the different needs of the sufferers.

Only one of the ten returns to thank the Giver of the miracle. Yes, and that one is the Samaritan. None of the Jews return. Full range of vocal powers had returned to the Samaritan and in a loud voice he glorified God, and falls down before Jesus expressing over and over the gratitude of his heart. No serious disappointment is in Jesus' voice as He asks, "Were there not ten cleansed, but where are the nine?" By failing to return, they showed that they thought more of themselves than of the Healer, which is typical, unfortunately, of so many who profit from the mercies of Christ. By their lack of appreciation they indicated that their Benefactor was no longer needed by them, because they were freed from their impediment.

35. Blind Bartimaeus

(Matthew 20:29–34; Mark 10:46–52; Luke 18:35–43)

Accompanied by His disciples and, of course, a large number of other people in orderly procession, Jesus was on His way to Jerusalem, for the last time! We didn't know, but Jesus knew that in less than a week His mission for His Father would be over. No doubt His sensitive spirit felt the weight of all that was to befall Him, yet such a burden did not stay His beneficial hand.

He had just left Jericho after being the guest of Zacchaeus. As we trudged along the road, a blind beggar inquired of the crowd the reason for such commotion. He was told that Jesus of Nazareth was passing by. Mark tells us that the conspicuous beggar was Bartimaeus, the son of Timaeus. Yes, Bartimaeus had heard about Jesus and His wonderful works, and now he takes advantage of the opportunity to call upon Him. He raised his voice and cried, "Jesus, Thou Son of David, have mercy on me!"

Being a beggar, he could have begged and received quite a bit of money from such a large crowd, but not this time. He was more interested in gaining eyesight. I thought that today many people are more interested in making more money than in thinking about their soul's salvation, failing to realize what a wonderful treasure they are sacrificing.

In his cry of naming Jesus "the Son of David," he signified acknowledgment of His Messiahship. The crowd rebuked Bartimaeus, but he was not to be silenced. He and his blind companion both cried out, "Have mercy upon us, O Lord!"

Jesus stood still and commanded above the rebuke noises of the crowd, "Be of good cheer, arise." Then Bartimaeus leaped up, flung off his outer garment of weather protection, and went toward Jesus. The ensuing question by Jesus is intriguing. He nearly always liked the needy to express their need and faith, though He knew what was needed. "What will ye have that I shall do unto you?" His question was intended, apparently, to evoke a livelier exercise of faith of the petitioner. There was no hesitation as to their expression of need, "Lord, that our eyes may be opened."

So Jesus touches their eyes and immediately they received sight. Their faith met the instant reward. Jesus said, "Thy faith hath saved thee." What a great outburst of gratitude for the cure, and they glorified God. They followed us then, as we continued toward Jerusalem, where Bartimaeus later appeared as a witness for the defense at our Lord's trial. Yes, you and I can see, as well as Bartimaeus, the glory of God in Jesus.

36. THE WITHERED FIG TREE

(Matthew 21:17–22; Mark 11:12–14)

NOW WE WILL SEE Jesus' only miracle of judgment. But before we watch this miracle let us consider His life in brief retrospect. Look at the life of deprivation He led in order to best serve His purpose in God's will. He found consolation, rest, and peace in Bethany with friends who were dear and close to Him. In His accepted poverty for our sake, Jesus became dependent upon others. He needed to be near friends. To understand this more, just take a look at His background. He was born in a stable, dined at others' tables much of the time, slept in borrowed or makeshift beds, and, as we shall see, He was buried in another man's grave.

We must keep in mind that Jesus was both divine and human. His humanity helped God better to understand mankind, his ego, his fluctuation in beliefs and attitude. By living as a man for a while, He and God could know humanity more completely.

Here we see Jesus starting for Jerusalem early in the morning without having eaten. As He walks along, hunger asserts itself and His human appetite arises. He sees a big fig tree up ahead by the road. Even though He has fed thousands previously, for Himself He would not perform a miracle to feed

Himself because it would not be serving others or glorifying God. Our Lord would not provide by miracle what could be provided by human endeavor or would not glorify God. But here He sees a big, beautiful tree with green leaves aplenty, but—no fruit! We were all disappointed. Christ stops and looks ahead at the city with pity. That city He had wept over, and soon would die in. All this realization moved Him to give a prophecy, a parable as a matter of fact. God came looking for the fruits of righteousness, but found nothing but the abundant leaves of a boastful yet empty endeavor by profession.

Finding no fruit, and acting with judgmental abruptness Jesus caused the tree to immediately wither, doomed to endless barrenness! Such action was not unjust, even though the tree was just a "thing," not a human. But by man it was used as a means for profitable ends. Christ did not attribute moral responsibilities to the tree when He smote it because of its unfruitfulness. He did, however, attribute to it an ability to represent moral quality, as a "good" tree, or a "bad" tree, or a tree that ought to bear fruit.

At this time of year, March or April, neither leaves nor fruit were naturally expected, but this tree, by putting forth leaves gave pretension to be something it wasn't, to have fruit since fruit is expected before leaves. Thus the disciples and others saw in the miracle God's abhorrence of hypocrisy, the cursing of a tree which boasted of having fruit, but not having fruit!

Cursing the fig tree was a symbolic action; for the tree represented Israel under the Old Covenant, soon to be utterly rejected as hopelessly unfruitful to God. The old way of changing and holding mankind in reverence and service to God had failed! Because of that fact Jesus was sent to earth! When God does not gather fruit from His ancient people, He will gather from a new arrangement under a Covenant of Grace, the New Testament. The withering of that tree was a result of Christ's faith in God, and used as a lesson for His disciples, that if they exercised a similar faith, power would be given to accomplish greater things.

37. THE MIRACLE OF MALCHUS' EAR

(Matthew 26:51–56; Mark 14:46,47; Luke 22:50,51; John 18:10,11)

AND NOW WE COME to the last recorded miracle by Christ. He has returned to the Garden of Gethsemane just outside of Jerusalem with great agony, distressful prayer, and bloody sweat. Jesus agonizes in prayer to His Father in Heaven while three of His disciples rest and sleep only a few yards away. Jesus walks back to where they are asleep, then returns to where He was and prayed some more. Then when God assured Him of what had to be, He was given Heavenly peace, then Jesus awakens the three and says, "Arise, let us be going." As they are leaving Gethsemane they are confronted by a multitude of people with swords and staves who had been sent out by the chief priest to take Jesus prisoner. Judas, the traitorous ex-disciple, had told where Jesus could be found, and now he approaches and gives Jesus a kiss on the cheek, the signal to the armed men that this is Jesus. Christ calmly asks, "Whom seek ye?" One of the men replies, "Jesus, the Nazarene." Jesus answers, "I am He." Jesus has no feeling of impending peril because He has chosen to yield to His captors.

Overcome by the majestic and quiet dignity, the crowd draws back and some fall to the ground. They are the ones who were afraid, not Jesus. They knew that Jesus' superior power could affect an escape. They were overcome, knowing His reputation, and seeing Him stand before them, devoid of any sign of fear. He could have walked away, but having been born to die as an atoning sacrifice, He meekly submitted Himself to His foes. He could have had "twelve legions of angels" to protect Him had He but asked for them; He desired only the fulfillment of God's plan.

The men arose to affect the capture. Seeing a man approach Jesus with sword in hand, Peter, the impetuous disciple, swings His own sword at the leader who ducks, and severs the ear of Malchus, a devout servant of the high priest. Malchus is startled and shocked as he puts his hand to his head. All action temporarily comes to a halt. Only two swords had been brought by the disciples and Peter has one of them. His action had been the impetuous move by an ardent, indignant man. Fortunately Malchus had ducked fast enough so that the sword missed its mark—his neck—and slid down the side of his face. If Peter had paused for a moment he would have known that armed resistance was hopeless against the well-armed contingent.

Jesus asks for one of His arms to be freed for just a moment. Look, He reaches up to the stunned man and touches his dangling ear. Lo, it is restored immediately! Can you imagine the amazement of Malchus as he reaches up to feel his restored ear? No pain remained, no damage at all. The ear is completely restored and healed!

This has been one of the few miracles that Jesus did without any expression or desire or faith from the recipient. This incident should be remembered. Jesus had come to lay down His life for sinners of the world, and in doing so He healed the wound of an antagonist. He disclosed His precept of loving His enemies. What amazing grace! I wonder if Malchus became a believer of Christ after this incident. The others must have also been divinely impressed.

Well, have you been seeing with the eyes of your heart? We have witnessed only a few of the miracles performed by Christ. As John had said, if all of them had been documented they would have filled untold numbers of volumes. How many people were healed by Christ in His three-year ministry? Thousands, don't you imagine?

38. AT CALVARY

COME, LET US SEE God's miraculous events that transpired at Calvary, or "Golgotha," which in Hebrew means "the place of the skull." On that small rocky mount, over there, just outside the wall of Jerusalem, is the place for crucifixions, the place of death for those criminals convicted of the worst crimes. After being "tried" by King Herod and the local Roman Emperor, Pilate, Jesus was sentenced to be crucified on a cross. He was not found guilty of anything, but was finally condemned because of the crowd's contemptuous demand for "crucifixion." Jesus was flogged, beaten, and made to drag the wooden cross from the court yard to Calvary among the jeers of a majority of Jews and then nailed to the cross between two criminals also on crosses.

Jesus' trial was a farce! Watch this. As soon as it was daylight that Friday, the elders of the people, the Chief Priest and the Scribes, met together, and then had Jesus brought into the Council. "Art thou the Christ? Tell us," He was asked. Jesus replied, "If I tell you, ye will not believe; and if I also ask you, ye will not answer Me, nor let Me go." Then they asked, "Art thou the Son of God?" And Christ said unto them, "Ye say that I am." Then it was agreed, "What need have we of any further witness for we ourselves have heard of his own mouth."

According to tradition, Pilate must release one prisoner at the time of the Passover. The crowd cries out in the Council Yard, "Away with this man, and release unto us Barabbas!" Pilate wanted to release Jesus, so he speaks once again to the mob, but they continue to cry out, "Crucify him, crucify him!" But then Pilate speaks to them the third time, "Why, what evil hath He done? I have found no cause for death in Him; I will therefore chastise Him, and let Him go!" But the crowd was instant with loud voices, demanding that he be crucified! Consequently, the will of the Chief Priests and their followers prevail, and Pilate passes the sentence. Barabbas, who was sentenced for sedition and murder, is released. *(Luke 23:17–25)*

The Roman Emperor, Pilate, wielded the power which condemned Jesus to death, though reluctantly. It was also a dream that Pilate's wife had. That dream brought a light from Heaven declaring the innocence of the one to be crucified. God, in His own way, conveyed his will directly, even to heathens like Pilate and his wife. That dream was a divine warning intended to save her husband from the guilt into which he was to plunge in order to please the people. Pilate also felt that Christ was innocent. His wife, legend affirms, became a convert to Christ, and perhaps so did Pilate.

Death on a cross was dealt to the worst criminals and slaves. Those condemned to death were scourged, beaten and stripped before being nailed to the cross with arms outstretched. Yet, when Jesus was condemned, the cross became the Christian symbol of all that is holy and precious to believers. By His dying on the "old rugged cross" He transformed its vile stature into exalted victory. Henceforth there are multitudes in Heaven and on earth who are rejoicing in the marvel of Divine Grace as shown on Calvary.

Because of the crucifixion, several other scriptures happened as predicted. The human suffering of Christ caused Him to cry out, "I thirst!" *(Psalm 69:21)* His death was near at hand. Another miracle of prophecy is seen when Christ was numbered with His transgressors. *(Isaiah 53:12)* Sometimes leg breaking was inflicted as a further punishment upon the victims, but was not done to Christ. His bones were spared when determined that He was already dead. *(Exodus 12:46; Numbers 9:12; Psalm 34:20)* Another scripture was also fulfilled when those around the cross gazed upon the victim; "They shall look on Him whom they have pierced." *(Zechariah 12:10)* A soldier drove a spear into Christ's side.

39. Jesus' Crucifixion

THE SUPERNATURAL SURROUNDED THE cross of Jesus, as darkness invaded the area that afternoon. It was almost like nighttime. There were many miracles of God that happened that fateful afternoon, but the greatest was the accomplishment of perfect salvation for the sinful lost. It took a miracle of God's grace to provide redemption for a world of sinners that had never been available under the law of the Old Covenant. The purpose of Jesus' death and God's miracles were to emancipate mankind from sin's penalty and power. Jesus fulfilled His mission and God's will on earth by paying with Jesus' blood as the last and permanent blood sacrifice for the redemption of mankind.

Jews, Roman soldiers, relatives and friends, looked upon Christ hanging nailed upon the cross.

The Jewish religious hierarchy wanted Jesus killed and disposed of before the beginning of the Sabbath day, which begins at 6:0 p.m. on Friday. Darkness has covered the land from noon until three in the afternoon. The darkness was nature's sympathy with her suffering Lord, and was another prophecy fulfillment. *(Amos 8:9)* The outward darkness, however, only symbolized the inner darkness Jesus was experiencing through the withdrawal of God's presence. None of us can know what He endured when He died as the substitute for sinners. In forlorn pain He cried, "My God, My God, why hast Thou forsaken Me?" A world of sin and God could not abide together in Jesus.

The earth was rent by a vicious earthquake at least twice and rocks were broken, but the crosses were unaffected. In the cemetery many graves were opened and the bodies of saints arose and walked the streets. They were some of those who had believed in Jesus during His ministry. Their sympathy was that great! As the earth was shaking the holy veil in the Temple was rent just as the Great High Priest was about to enter. The veil was torn from the top all the way to the bottom, meaning, of course, that it was rent by God and not by man. That huge veil was believed to be a hand-breadth in thickness and was woven of seventy-two twisted plaits, each plait consisting of twenty-four threads. It was sixty feet long and thirty feet wide. Two more threads were added every year. The veil was opened only once a year when only the High Priest was permitted to enter into the room of holiest holy to talk to God. Each time it took about 400 priests to manipulate the opening of the veil because of its great weight. Thus, by tearing the veil open, the barrier between God and man was done away with. The Temple and its old ceremonial form of worship were no longer needed. A new way of worship of God was opened into the presence of God, open to any person, who believes in Jesus, can talk to God in prayer. From that moment the cross became the way which admitted man to the Holy Place, according to the believing relationship in Christ. *(Hebrews 9:8, 10:19–31)* Ambrose, in an ancient hymn, expressed it: "When Thou didst overcome the sharpness of death, Thou didst open the Kingdom of Heaven to all believers."

John watched as the Roman soldier walked up to the cross and pierced Jesus' side with his spear. He later related the incident with the solemn affirmation and authority of the eye witness. Water and blood flowed from the pierced side. At the same time a giant tidal wave affected the waters and rose high in the rivers and estuaries. How symbolic that was, for on that day the abounding Grace of God rose high above the mighty obstacles of human sin and became destined to lift the entire universe of men nearer to God, who through the cross will reconcile all things to Himself, whether in Heaven or on earth.

Jesus exercised the prerogative of deity even in the agonies of death. He could have saved Himself form those agonies, but because He was the Son of God, He did not have the right to save Himself. See, if he had done so, there would have been no salvation for you and me. His believers urged Him to come down from the cross, and by such show of power prove beyond any doubt that He was God, but it was ordained that deity should die for us. As Redeemer He had to drain the cup to its bitter dregs. Before He died, He manifested His divine power in the pardon of the dying thief on the cross next to Him. That thief was the first trophy of the efficacy of His shed blood. In the moment of His greatest weakness he was able to save the repentant soul who had turned to Him for forgiveness. Jesus told him that he would be with Him this day in Paradise.

The Roman centurion in charge of the crucifixion looked up at the man on the middle cross, and said, "Truly this was the Son of God." How true it is that His cross draws all mankind unto Him. Jesus willingly gave up His life on earth. Both His death and resurrection were at His command in order to serve the purpose for which He came to earth, to offer to those of us who would believe, the "only way" to have eternal life with Him in glory.

40. THE RESURRECTION

THE MIRACLE OF HIS resurrection was the crowning achievement of His coming to earth. Death could not keep its prey. He arose, and He lives today! "I lay down My life that I may take it up again." His empty tomb demonstrated the fulfillment of that prediction. He is risen! The body of Gautama Buddha, the founder of Buddhism, was burnt after his death; that of Mohamet was buried in Mecca; and that of Confucius in his family village. No affirmation of resurrection is associated with those or any other founders of religions—except Jesus Christ!

The soldiers found that Jesus was already dead when they carried out the act of breaking the legs of those two who were still alive. All were removed from the crosses. A well-to-do man, and believer, named Joseph of Arimathia, gave permission for his tomb to be used for Jesus in the nearby garden at the foot of the Calvary Mount. It was at that moment when Christ died yet another earthquake hit and it was then that the veil in the temple was rent. Some women were watching the crucifixion from a distance, such as Mary Magdalene, and Mary, the mother of Jesus, standing with John the disciple. Earlier it was John to whom Jesus spoke, "Here is your mother," and to Mother Mary He said, "Dear woman, here is your son," referring to John. From that time on, the disciple took widow Mary into his home.

Joseph of Arimathea, a respected member of the very council which had pressed for Jesus' execution, had asked for the body and had had it placed in his own tomb. *(Matthew 27:25; Mark 15;42–45)* It was Nicodemus, the Pharisee and Jewish ruler who had gone to Jesus by night asking how one could be born again, who helped move Jesus to the tomb. Those two men, whose lives had been so touched by Jesus, showed their gratitude in that way in final tribute.

Taking the body, the two of them wrapped it with strips of linen and applied some spices. They had brought about seventy-five pounds of mixture composed of myrrh and aloe. Joseph and Nicodemus placed the body in the new tomb which had been carved out of the rock embankment. *(Matthew 27:61; Mark 15:47)* Jesus' body was placed on the resting place, a horizontally carved rock about eighteen inches high. Jesus was about six feet tall, but fit the tomb slab quite well. Joseph and Nicodemus, along with a couple of onlookers, rolled the stone, which weighed about a ton, over the doorway. The women from Galilee followed Joseph and saw how the body was laid, then they went home, crying, to start preparing spices and perfumes. *(Matthew 27:62–66)*

The Chief Priests and some Pharisees went to Pilate, saying, "Sir, we remember that when He was still alive the deceiver said, 'After three days I will rise again.' Give the order for the tomb to be made secure until the third day at least, otherwise His disciples may come and steal the body and tell the people that He has risen from the dead. This last deception will be worse than the first." *(Matthew 27:62–66)*

"Take a guard." Pilate answered. "Go, make the tomb secure as you know how." So they went and secured the tomb by putting a seal on the stone and posting guards.

The events which follow are certainly miraculous, as you will see. They only confirm Jesus' credibility and provide believers the assurance of His life after death. *(Matthew 28:1–10; Mark 16:1–11; Luke 24:1–12; John 20:1–8; Corinthians 15:4–8)*

On Sunday morning there was another violent earthquake. An angel of the Lord came down from Heaven, went to the tomb, rolled back the stone from the doorway and sat upon it. His appearance was very bright, and his clothes were as white as snow. The guards were so afraid of him that they shook and became as immobile as dead men. They soon recovered, however, and ran to tell the authorities what had happened.

Later that Sunday morning Mary Magdalene, Salome, and Mother Mary brought spices to anoint Jesus' body. On the way they asked each other, "Who will roll the stone away from the tomb?" Then they saw, to their amazement, that the stone had already been rolled away! They were startled to see the young man in white sitting on the stone. They went ahead and entered the tomb, but were startled again to see another man in white sitting on the right side of the slab where Jesus' head would be.

41. POST-RESURRECTION

(Matthew 16:1–4; Luke 24:2)

"DON'T BE ALARMED," THE angel said. "You are looking for Jesus the Nazarene, who was crucified? He has risen! He is not here. See the place where they laid Him. But go, tell His disciples and Peter. He is going ahead of you into Galilee. There you will see Him, just as He told you." While they stood there pondering, suddenly two men stood before them in snow white clothes gleaming like lightning. In their fright the women bowed down with their faces toward the ground, then one of the men said to them, "Why do you look for the living among the dead? He is not here; He has risen." Then, trembling and bewildered, the women went out from the tomb. They said nothing to anyone because they were afraid. Mary Magdalene went running ahead to Simon Peter and told him what had happened. Both he and John ran to the tomb, John arriving first. Inside he saw the strips of linen lying there. "The napkin that was upon His head was rolled or coiled up in 'a place by itself.'" John's sharp eye had noticed that. Had the body been stolen, it is unlikely that the linens would have been neatly folded and left behind. The long strip of linen was lying exactly in the same position they had seen three days before.

Mary Madgalene had also returned and stood outside the

tomb crying. Then she also went inside and saw the two angels in white sitting where Jesus' body had been, one sitting at the head, one at the foot.

They asked her, "Woman, why are you crying?"

"They have taken my Lord away," she said, "and I don't know where they have put Him!" At that point she went outside, still weeping. Then she saw a man there in the garden whom she assumed to be the gardener.

"Woman," he said, "Why are you crying? Who is it you are looking for?"

Mary said, "Sir, if you have carried Him away, tell me where you have put Him, and I will get Him."

"Mary," Jesus said!

Startled, she cried out in Aramaic, "Rabboni," meaning teacher.

Jesus calmly said to her, "Do not hold onto Me, for I have not yet returned to the Father. Go instead to My brothers and tell them, I am returning to My Father and your Father, to My God and your God."

The two other women were astounded at what they and we just saw, and they were joyously happy! They hurried away from the garden, afraid and yet filled with joy, and they went on their way to tell the other disciples.

Some of the guards had gone into the city. Everything was reported to the Priests. They, of course, could not believe that it had happened as reported. They huddled together and devised a plan. They gave the guards large sums of money and instructed them, "You are to say, his disciples came during the night and stole him away while we slept. If this report gets to the governor, we will satisfy him and keep you out of trouble." So the soldiers did as they were paid to do. So this story was widely circulated among the Jews, and believed by most, even to this day.

As the women were on their way to tell the disciples what had happened, suddenly Jesus miraculously appeared before them!

"Greetings," He said to the startled women. They went to Him and clasped His feet, and worshipped Him. Then Jesus said, "Do not be afraid. Go and tell My brothers (disciples) to go to Galilee; there they will see Me."

They wasted no time in getting to the eleven. Judas, of course, was no longer with them as he had hanged himself after having turned Jesus over to the authorities. Well, the women reported to them all the details. There also were others, namely Joanna, Mother Mary, and several others who had joined them. Of course all could not believe what they were told. It seemed so incredible! Nevertheless, the men made ready to set out for Galilee, muttering to each other.

On that same day, about an hour later, two of the newer followers of Jesus were on the road to Emmaus after leaving Jerusalem on their way home. They were occupied in talking about the crucifixion. As they were covering the seven mile distance Jesus Himself came onto the road, caught up with them, and asked them what they were talking about. They didn't recognize who it was because they were so absorbed in their thoughts and conversation. They paused, their faces still downcast, and one of them, Cleopas, asked Him, "Are you only a visitor to Jerusalem and do not know what happened there in the last few days?"

"What things?" He asked.

"About Jesus of Nazareth," he explained. He went on to tell about how Jesus, a prophet in word and deed before God and all the people, had been killed. The Chief Priests and rulers had handed Him over to be sentenced to death, and He was crucified. It was hoped that He was the Messiah, at last. Now it is the third day since He was killed, and can you imagine, some of our women went to the tomb this morning and found the tomb empty! The body was gone! Well, we were told that there were a couple of angles there who said that Jesus is alive! Some of our companions also went to the tomb and found it just as the women had said, but they couldn't find Jesus or His body anywhere."

Jesus said to them, "How foolish you are, and how slow of heart to believe all that the prophets have spoken. Did not Christ have to suffer these things and then to enter glory?" He then explained to them about Moses and all the prophets and what was said in their scriptures concerning Jesus, the Messiah.

As they arrived in Emmasus, Jesus acted as though He intended to go on, but they asked Him to come in, since it was almost evening. So He went in with them and, when they sat at the table, Jesus took the bread, gave thanks, broke it and passed it to them. Then, suddenly, their eyes were opened and they recognized Him. As they looked aghast at Him, Jesus began to fade from their sight!

They immediately got up from the table and hurried back to Jerusalem. There in the evening of the first day of the week, Sunday, the disciples were met together behind locked doors, as was their practice. They were all set to go to Galilee. Cleopas and his friend were admitted and told them what had happened on the road, and how Jesus was there with them and how they finally recognized Him when He broke bread. Those ten men, and those with them, smiled and said, "Then it is true! The Lord has risen and has also appeared to Simon."

While they were all still talking amongst themselves, Jesus suddenly stood before them, and said to them in greeting, "Peace be with you." *(Mark 16:14; Luke 24:36–44; John 20:20)*

They were startled and frightened, thinking they were seeing a ghost. He said to them, "Why are you troubled, and why do doubts rise in your minds? Look at My hands and My feet. It is I Myself! Touch Me and see, a ghost does not have flesh and bones, as you see I have."

They still found it difficult to believe what they wer seeing. They were filled with amazement, as were we, and with joy at the same time!

He asked, "Do you have anything here to eat?" They handed Him a piece of broiled fish. He took it and ate it in their presence.

He said to them, "This is what I told you while I was still with you. Everything must be fulfilled that is written about Me in the law of Moses, the Prophets and the Psalms."

Again Jesus spoke, "Peace be with you! As the Father has sent Me, I am sending you." *(John 20:21–23)* And with that He breathed on them and said, "Receive the Holy Spirit. If you forgive anyone his sins, they are forgiven; if you do not forgive them, they are not forgiven."

Thomas, one of the disciples, was not with the others when Jesus appeared before them. When told of it later, he said that he couldn't believe it. *(John 20:24–25)* "Unless I see the nail marks in His hands and put my finger where the nails were, and put my hand into His side, I will not believe it."

A week later, when the disciples had met again in the room, Thomas was with them. Though the doors were closed and locked, Jesus appeared and stood before them and said, "Peace be with you." (or "Shalom" in Hebrew, which is a greeting.) Turning to Thomas, He said, "Put your finger here; see My hands. Reach out your hand and put it into My side. Stop doubting and believe." (He could be saying the same to you and me.)

Thomas said, "My Lord and My God!"

Jesus told him, "Because you have seen Me, you have believed; blessed are those who have not seen and yet have believed.

42. POST-RESURRECTION MIRACLE
OF THE FISHES

(John 21:1–13)

JESUS HAD REQUESTED THAT His disciples go ahead to Galilee and that He would meet them there. Now look at this! Jesus appears and walks toward the shore line of the Lake of Tiberias. This happens to be the last miracle Jesus performs before His ascension. The disciples, however, had not waited around doing nothing. They had boarded Peter's boat and gone out for a little fishing, for they knew that Jesus would have no difficulty in finding them.

It was still early morning when they were nearing the shore, devoid of any fish. Jesus was there standing at the landing, but the disciples did not recognize Him in the subdued light. Jesus called, "Children, have you any meat?" When the answer was "no," He said, "Cast the net on the right side of the ship, and ye shall find." They did so, still not recognizing that the "stranger" was really the Lord. They immediately caught a tremendous load of fish. The Almighty One knew where the fish were, and He could direct them into the net. Such a display of omniscience and power revealed to John who the stranger was. He exclaimed to Peter, "It is the Lord!"

When Peter realized this, he put on his outer fisherman's coat and plunged into the water and waded to be the first to greet Jesus! The boat was brought in, dragging the full load of fish. What a happy event had just happened, and what a surprise still awaited them on shore! A hot breakfast of fish and bread was ready for them because Jesus had personally prepared it. We are not told "how" the meal was prepared, but without the 153 fish just brought in, Jesus had cooked fish ready to be eaten. By the way, it was much later discovered that the different species of fish in the lake were exactly 153. In other words, the catch contained one of each kind of fish that Jesus had directed into the net.

With a nice invitation from Jesus saying, "Come and dine," they joined Him. He took the bread and fish, blessed them, and then passed them to His disciples. There was something mysterious and majestic about His form, rather felt than seen.

This was the third time that Jesus had shown Himself to His disciples after His resurrection. When they had dined, Jesus asked Peter, "Simon, son of Jonas, lovest Me more than these?" "Yes, Lord, Thou knowest that I love Thee." Jesus said in all sincerity, "Feed My lambs." A little while later He asked the same question. Peter answered in the same way, and Jesus again said, "Feed My sheep." But when Jesus asked the same question for the third time, Peter was getting a little peeved. He replied, "Lord, Thou knowest all things. Thou knowest that I love Thee." And for the third time Jesus said, "Feed my sheep." A moment later He said, "Follow Me."

Don't you know that the disciples felt deep in their hearts the true significance of the repeated question from their Lord. Did they not discern that in His closing time with them, He was preparing them to carry forth His commission of going into all the world to preach the redeeming Gospel which He made possible by His death and resurrection? *(Matthew 28:16–20)*

Then Jesus said to them, "All authority in Heaven and earth has been given Me. Therefore go and make disciples of all nations; baptizing them in the name of the Father and the Son and of the Holy Spirit, and teaching them to obey everything I have commanded of you. And surely I am with you always, to the very end of the age. Whoever believes and is baptized will be saved, but whoever does not believe will be condemned. (Remember that! One has to believe in Jesus Christ as Lord and Savior.) And these signs will accompany those who believe. In My name they will drive out demons."

Some time passed before Jesus met with His disciples for the last time in their room. During His thirty-nine-day presence on earth after resurrection, Jesus was seen by approximately 500 people. *(Luke 24:45–49)*

Jesus gave parting instructions to His apostles there in Jerusalem before Pentecost, the annual Harvest Festival. He opened their minds so they could understand the scriptures. He told them, "This is what is written: The Christ will suffer and rise from the dead on the third day, and repentance and forgiveness of sins will be preached in His name to all nations, beginning in Jerusalem. You are witnesses of these things; I am going to send you what My Father promised; but stay in the city until you have been clothed with power on high." *(Mark 16:19; Luke 24:50, 51; Acts 1:6–11)*

When Jesus had led them out to the vicinity toward Bethany, He lifted up His hands and blessed them. They asked Him, "Lord, are you at this time going to restore the Kingdom to Israel?" He said to them, "It is not for you to know the time or dates the Father has set by His own authority. But you will receive power when the Holy Spirit comes to you; and you will be My witnesses in Jerusalem, and in all Judea and Samaria, and to the ends of the earth." The apostles were given the power when the Holy Spirit came upon them ten days later, on Pentecost.

43. Jesus' Ascension

(Luke 24:52; Acts 1:12–14)

B EHOLD, WILL YOU! HERE near Bethany Jesus is taken up right
before the very eyes of us and His apostles! You can't forget
this sight, ever. He was on a cloud as He arose, then the cloud
hid Him from our view. Look, the apostles stand around, spell-
bound, looking up into the sky where He disappeared.
Suddenly, two men dressed in snow white clothes stood beside
them! "Men of Galilee," one of the men said. "Why do you
stand there looking into the sky? This same Jesus who has been
taken from you into Heaven, will come back in the same way
you have seen Him go into Heaven."

Then all of the apostles worshipped Him and returned to
Jerusalem with great joy! When they arrived there, most of
them went upstairs to the room where they were staying. Those
known to be present were Peter, John, James, Andrew, and
Simon the Zealot, and also Judas the son of James. They all
joined together constantly in prayer, along with the women
who were there, and Mary the Mother of Jesus, and His brothers.

The apostles were so called because their training under
Jesus was completed, and they were left to carry on with the
missionary work as instructed by Jesus. They were God's cho-

sen representatives, consecrated to His cause, and infused with the Holy Spirit. They were never alone, as God was with them in all that they did and said, every step of the way. Their status is the same as those of us who believe in Jesus as Lord and Savior. You, too, will become aware of this as time goes by.

Yes, our Lord, Jesus Christ, is alive. He arose from the dead, assuring you and me that we will do the same, only if we believe in Him. In a little over a month after being raised from the dead, Jesus appeared to more than 550 people.

He appeared to Mary Magdalene at the tomb *(John 20:11–18)* and to three or four other women returning to the tomb *(Matthew 28:9–10)*. He appeared on the road to Emmaus beside two disciples *(Luke 24:13–32)* and later to Simon Peter *(Luke 24:34)*. He went into the upper room to the ten disciples on Resurrection Day. *(John 20:19–23; Luke 24:36–43)*. A week later He returned to them again when "doubting" Thomas was there. And there on the shore of Galilee, Jesus prepared breakfast for seven disciples *(John 21:1–23)*. He appeared before more than 500 people in Galilee for the "Great Commission." *(Matthew 28:16–20; Mark 16:15; Corinthians 15:6)*. He came before His brother, James *(I Corinthians f15:7)*. And finally to all the disciples at His ascension into a cloud *(Luke 24:44–53; Acts 1:1–9)*.

Then, in a brilliant light and in speech, He appointed Paul as a disciple on the road to Damascus. After John had been arrested and exiled to the Isle of Patmos, He also appeared and inspired John to write the Book of Revelation *(1:9–20)*.

44. Peter Proclaims Jesus as Christ

(Acts 2:14–36)

TEN DAYS AFTER JESUS' ascension, at Pentecost, a great spiritual victory was had when all the apostles taught multitudes of people. So endowed were they with the "Holy Spirit," God's universal omnipotent presence in the Christian Apostles, that they spoke to all nations represented there so that those peoples heard the message in their own language. Amazing!

Peter spoke: "Men of Israel, listen to this: Jesus of Nazareth was a man accredited by God to you by miracles, wonders, and signs, which God did among you through Him, as you yourselves know. This man was handed over to you by god's set purpose and foreknowledge, and you, with the help of wicked men, put Him to death by nailing Him to the cross. But God raised Him from the dead, freeing Him from agony of death, because it was impossible for death to keep its hold on Him!"

"Therefore let all Israel be assured of this: God has made this Jesus, whom you crucified, both Lord and Christ."

When the people heard this, they were cut to the heart and said to Peter and the other apostles, "Brothers, what shall we do?" *(Acts 2:37–41)*

Peter replied, "Repent and be baptized, every one of you, in the name of Jesus Christ for the forgiveness of your sins, and you will receive the gift of the Holy Spirit. The promise is for you and your children and for all who are far off—for all the Lord our God will call."

As the result of the ministry that day, over three thousand people were saved and baptized!

A strong fellowship of Christian believers was formed as a family of God, and the Lord added to their number daily, those who were saved.

Saul came along later. He had been a persecutor of Christians for the Jewish High Priests. He was feared by all who regarded the name of Jesus as precious. He was assigned to persecute and arrest all those who believed in Jesus and he was on his way to Damascus to bring prisoners back to Jerusalem. Suddenly a bright light from Heaven shown about Him,, and the men with him! Saul fell to the ground, blinded! To him Jesus spoke, "I am Jesus whom you are persecuting. Now get up and go into the city, and you will be told what to do."

The Lord also spoke to a disciple in Damascus, named Ananias, and told him that Paul (name changed by Jesus) would arrive as God's chosen instrument to carry His gospel to the Gentiles. There in the city Paul regained his sight, was baptized and became a devout Christian.

Paul ministered faithfully as a great apostle to many nations. A fellow by the name of Matthias became the twelfth apostle, replacing the traitor Judas. Thus, with the selection of Paul, Christianity had a great working force not just in Israel but also in adjacent nations.

45. How One Becomes a Christian

M Y FRIEND YOU HAVE witnessed the miracles of God through Jesus, and have walked with the Christ as He ministered to the Holy Land. "You have seen with your heart." *(Colossians 1:29–31)*

Now it should be seen clearly by you that Jesus was God's solution to the increasing and perpetual problem of sin, and man's lack of faith, and his disobedience to God's will. As promised through God's prophecy, Christ, the "King" came to change the religious system of old and to deliver man from sin by living in him as the Holy Spirit. Christ provided the way for permanent redemption and forgiveness by His death and resurrection. *(Galatians 3:13)* He died for all that those who believe should not henceforth live unto themselves, but unto Him who died for them, and rose again. *(Corinthians 5:15)* By His resurrection from the dead, He insures our rise from the dead also.

"Therefore if any man be in Christ, he is a new creature: old things are passed away; behold, all things are become new!" *(Corinthians 5:17, 18)*

When one becomes a Christian, he is overwhelmed by joy in being born again through Christ.

"And all things are of God, who hath reconciled us to Himself by Christ, and hath given us the ministry of reconciliation." *(Corinthians 5:18)*

"To wit that God was in Christ, reconciling the world unto Himself, not imputing their trespasses unto them; and hath committed unto us the Word of reconciliation." *(Corintians 5:19)*, written by the Apostle Paul.

"And as Christians: Now that we are ambassadors for Christ, as from God, did beseech you by us; we pray you in Christ's stead, be ye reconciled to God." *(Corinthians 5:20)*

"Christ is the image of the invisible God, the firstborn over all creation. For by Him all things were created; things in rulers and authorities; all things were created by Him and for Him. He is before all things, and in Him all things hold together." *(Collossians 1:15–20)*

It is so easy to become a Christian! First, you see, because you, like everyone, have sinned, and have come short of the glory of God.

A person who does not believe in things we have seen, is condemned already. Whenever he does believe that Jesus is Lord and Savior, then he becomes saved.

For your sins, you must sincerely repent. How? You simply pray to God, in Jesus' name, confessing all your sins. He hears, if you are truly sincere. Its just between you and God.

If you are honestly sincere, suddenly God will forgive you of "all" your sins, and you will be saved! It is so simple, yet it is the most precious gift you can receive. You will immediately receive God's Holy Spirit! He will thusly live in your heart for the rest of your life on earth. You will have Heavenly Peace in your heart, even while going through life's troubles, and you will smile as you win. Furthermore, you will have God's guidance and help. He will always be on your side against the devil and anything he may throw at you.

"When God, our Savior, appeared, He saved, not because of righteous things we have done, but because of His mercy. He saved us through the washing of rebirth and renewal by the Holy Spirit." *(Titus 3:3–8)*

When you have done this, at last you can breathe deeply, and

thank God for His precious gift to you. Simply by believing in
Jesus Christ you are saved, and you will have everlasting life
with Him in His glorious Heavenly Kingdom!

Heaven after life on earth is promised to you, simply by
believing in what we have seen, and by asking to be forgiven of
your sins! How wonderful! How simple!

We are almost back to the hotel, and our tour is coming to
an end. It has been a pleasure to have you go around the Holy
Land, walking with Jesus. Though it is tiresome, you will never
grow tired of living with Him through the eternal presence of
the Holy Spirit. Believe and trust in God and you will live a
happy life, even though you may be poor. "Whatever happens,
conduct yourself in a manner worthy of the gospel of Christ."
(Philippians 1:21–23)

Jesus lives! We have seen Him here on earth thirteen different times after His resurrection from the dead. Upon leaving in
the cloud, we were promised that the Messiah will return to
gather to Himself all those who believed in Him. You will savor
the life you have, because you will live in Jesus.

Wherever you go, and if you meet a lost and sinful man, you
can tell him these few steps he can take to be saved:

> 1. He that believeth not is condemned already,
> because he hath not believed in the name of
> the only begotten Son of God. *(John 3:18)*

> 2. Jesus answering said unto them, ..."except ye
> repent, ye shall all likewise perish." *(Luke 13:3)*

> 3. "For God so loved the world, that He gave
> His only begotten Son, that whosoever
> believeth in Him should not perish, but have
> everlasting life." *(John 3:16)*

> 4. "Whosoever therefore shall confess me
> before men, him will I confess before My
> Father which is in Heaven." *(Matthew 10:32)*

5. Jesus answered and said, ..."if a man love Me, he will keep My words." *(John 14:23)*

Now, "Put on full armor of God so that you can take your stand against the devil's schemes...stand firm then, with the belt of truth buckled around your waist, with the breastplate of righteousness in its place, and with your feet fitted with readiness that comes from the gospel of Peace." *(Ephesians 6:10–17)*

Death on a cross was dealt to the worst criminals and slaves. Those condemned to death on the cross were scourged, beaten and stripped before being nailed to the cross with arms outstretched. Yet, because Jesus was thus condemned, the cross has become the symbol of all that is holy and precious to believers. By His dying on the "old rugged cross," He transformed its vile stature into exaulted victory. Henceforth, there are multitudes in Heaven and on earth who are rejoicing in the marvel of divine grace as shown on Calvary.

The Roman procurator of Judea, Pontius Pilate, was the power which condemned Jesus to death, though reluctantly. It was in a dream that Pilate's wife came to believe as actions continued toward the destruction of Jesus. That dream brought a light from Heaven declaring the innocence of the One to be crucified. God, in His own way, conveyed His will directly, even to heathens like Pilate and his wife. That dream was a divine warning intended to save her husband, who also believed in Christ's innocence, from the guilt and sin into which he was to plunge in order to please the people. His wife, legend affirms, became a convert to Christ, and perhaps so did Pilate.

Several prophecies of ancient scriptures were happening as predicted. The human suffering of Christ caused Him to cry out, "I thirst!" *(Psalm 69:21)* His death was near at hand. Another miracle of prophecy is seen when Christ was numbered with His transgressors. *(Isaiah 53:12)* Sometimes legbreaking was inflicted as a further punishment upon slaves, but was not wrought upon Jesus. His bones were spared when determined that He was already dead. *(Exodus 12:46; Numbers 9:12; Psalm 34:20)* Another scripture was fulfilled when those around the cross gazed upon the victim, "They shall look on

Him whom they have pierced." *(Zechariah 12:10)* A soldier drove a spear into Christ's side.

46. The Shroud of Turin

Now before we part and start packing for our departure from the Holy Land, let me tell you also about the Shroud of Turin. In addition to my painting done from my dream description (see postscript), and the letter written by the Roman, Publius Lentulus, there exists a third description of Jesus' appearance, the Shroud of Turin. Strangely enough, all three descriptions thoroughly agree.

The Shroud was found about 600 years ago. Documented is the fact that around 1350 Geoffrey the First of Charnes, a famous French Knight of the period, presented the linen cloth to the church in Lirey, France, claiming it was the burial cloth of Jesus.

It came into the possession of the House of Savoy, the exiled family of Italy, in 1578. From that time it has been kept under lock and key in the Cathedral of Turin, accounting for its name.

The photographs of the Shroud clearly show the portrait of a bearded man with long hair and a majestic expression. The Shroud's authenticity is further supported by the location of bloodstains on the cloth. Distinct stains can be seen around the head, and also around the hands and feet. There is also a stain of clotted blood below a wound-mark on the right side of the chest, where Christ was pierced by a spear.

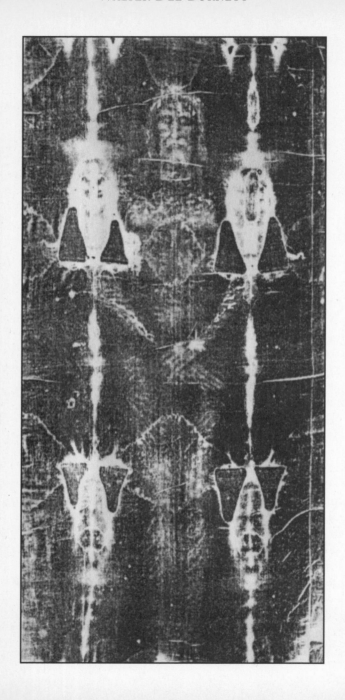

Much debate has developed as to how the finely detailed image of a man's face could appear on the cloth. Now a Russian biochemist says that the results of radiocarbon are wrong because scientists failed to take into account the effects on the Shroud of a fire that had scorched the material in the sixteenth century and altered the radiocarbon calculations. When the

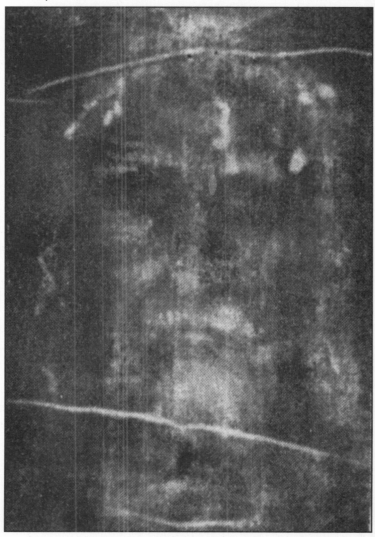

mathematical adjustments were made, the exact age of the Shroud was determined to be 1,800 years or more, placing it back in the time of Christ.

A Vatican archivist maintains that the image is the result of chemical actions of the myrrh and powder in reaction with the body sweat chemicals. Ordinarily a dying person would not sweat so profusely as to set the oxidation process in motion, but one pathologist says that a man in crisis of pain, as was the case with Christ carrying all the sins of the world, and having been tortured such a length of time, would be quite sweaty. One theory contends the Shroud's image was made by an electrical dischard at the moment of resurrection. Such was possible, because virtually everything Christ did was supernatural.

Hence we have the only three descriptions of how our Lord, Jesus Christ, looked. He, therefore, gave us the only descriptions, and that is enough. His actual image does not matter. Various people may have different ideas as to how Jesus looked, and that is each person's prerogative. All that really matters is that Jesus Christ existed then, and he lives now.

So, here we are back at the hotel, bringing to an end a wonderful tour with you. I have enjoyed being with you and I hope you enjoyed the tour also. Just remembering the full life of Jesus on earth that we witnessed fills my heart with joy and peace.

May God bless you always…"having been buried with Him in Baptism, and raised through faith in the power of God who raised Him from the dead." *(Colossians 29:15)*

As you now know…
this is not the end,
but the beginning!!

POSTSCRIPT

THE PORTRAIT ON THE cover resulted from my being blessed by a dream one night. I, Walter Dee Burnett, had a Heavenly Dream. It was about three o'clock that night when I had the clearest of all dreams. I was suspended at night about twelve feet off the ground. There before me was what looked like a highway covered lightly with a gray dust. I thought at the time that it was a covering of fallout from a nuclear explosion. Suspended on the other side of the highway, at about the same height as I, was a long row of framed oil paintings well illuminated. Standing on the ground was a bearded man, clad in a robe, who was looking at the paintings as they slowly moved forward toward him one at a time. He was someone who had known Jesus Christ very well. I supposed he was Simon Peter, the disciple of Jesus.

The sky was apparently filled with people, or angels, and though I saw no one, I could hear them talking. Peter was judging the many paintings done by all the world's artists since the time of Jesus' Ascension into Heaven. He, who had known Jesus best, was to find the painting that looked the most like Jesus Christ, our Lord and Savior. He looked at each painting, one after the other. As he looked he would slowly shake his head and the painting would fall away, disintegrating before it hit the ground. He paced to and fro as he carefully appraised each painting. Then I was startled by the next one that came up. I leaned forward and looked, and, yes, the signature element in the lower right hand corner was mine, "Burnett, 1986."

Peter pondered with his hand to his chin, then slowly nodded his head. All the paintings, except mine, fell away and disintegrated. There was much applauding and shouting by the angels! They all knew Jesus and they agreed with the judge's selection!